The Nurse's
Meditative Journal

The Nurse's Meditative Journal

SHERRY KAHN, MPH

Health educator, communications consultant, longtime meditator, and explorer of a variety of spiritual traditions. Ms. Kahn is the coauthor of *Healing Yourself: A Nurse's Guide to Self-Care and Renewal* (Delmar, 1994), a principal editor at UCLA Medical Center, and president of *Self-Care for Caregivers* — continuing education workshops, retreats, and materials — Los Angeles, California. Ms. Kahn also holds a master's degree in public health and a bachelor of science in zoology.

Delmar Publishers

I(T)P™ **An International Thomson Publishing Company**

Albany • Bonn • Boston • Cincinnati • Detroit • London • Madrid • Melbourne
Mexico City • New York • Pacific Grove • Paris • San Francisco • Singapore • Tokyo
Toronto • Washington

NOTICE TO THE READER

Cover Design: Spiral Design
Cover Illustration: Kirsten Soderlind

Delmar Staff

Publisher: Diane L. McOscar
Senior Acquisitions Editor: Bill Burgower
Senior Marketing Manager: Hank Bertsch
Assistant Editor: Debra M. Flis
Project Editor: Judith Boyd Nelson
Production Coordinator: Barbara A. Bullock
Art and Design Coordinator: Mary E. Siener
Editorial Assistant: Chrisoula Baikos

COPYRIGHT © 1996
By Delmar Publishers
a division of International Thomson Publishing Inc.

The ITP logo is a trademark under license.

Printed in the United States of America

For more information, contact:

Delmar Publishers
3 Columbia Circle, Box 15015
Albany, New York 12212-5015

International Thomson Publishing Europe
Berkshire House 168-173
High Holborn
London, WC1V 7AA
England

Thomas Nelson Australia
102 Dodds Street
South Melbourne, 3205
Victoria, Australia

Nelson Canada
1120 Birchmont Road
Scarborough, Ontario
Canada, M1K 5G4

International Thomson Editores
Campos Eliseos 385, Piso 7
Col Polanco
11560 Mexico D F Mexico

International Thomson Publishing GmbH
Konigswinterer Strasse 418
53227 Bonn
Germany

International Thomson Publishing Asia
221 Henderson Road
#05-10 Henderson Building
Singapore 0315

International Thomson Publishing—Japan
Hirakawacho Kyowa Building, 3F
2-2-1 Hirakawacho
Chiyoda-ku, Tokyo 102
Japan

1 2 3 4 5 6 7 8 9 10 XXX 01 00 99 98 97 96 95

Library of Congress Cataloging-in-Publication Data

Kahn, Sherry.
   The nurse's meditative journal / Sherry Kahn.
      p.   cm. — (Nurse as healer series)
   Includes bibliographical references.
   ISBN 0-8273-7109-8 (alk. paper)
   1. Nurses—Psychology. 2. Meditation—Therapeutic use.
3. Diaries—Therapeutic use. 4. Stress management. I. Title.
II. Series.
   [DNLM: 1. Nurses—psychology. 2. Relaxation Techniques—nurses'
instruction. 3. Writing—nurses' instruction. 4. Stress,
Psychological—prevention & control—nurses' instruction. WY 87
K12n 1996]
RT86.K343 1996
610.73—dc20
DNLM/DLC
for Library of Congress

94-36263
CIP

INTRODUCTION TO NURSE AS HEALER SERIES

LYNN KEEGAN, PhD, RN, Series Editor

Associate Professor, School of Nursing,
University of Texas Health Science Center at San Antonio
San Antonio, Texas
and Director of BodyMind Systems, Temple, Texas

To nurse means to care for or to nurture with compassion. Most nurses begin their formal education with this ideal. Many nurses retain this orientation after graduation, and some manage their entire careers under this guiding principle of caring. Many of us, however, tend to forget this ideal in the hectic pace of our professional and personal lives. We may become discouraged and feel a sense of burnout.

Throughout the past decade I have spoken at hundreds of conferences with thousands of nurses. Their experience of frustration and failure is quite common. These nurses feel themselves spread as pawns across a health care system too large to control or understand. In part, this may be because they have forgotten their true roles as nurse-healers.

When individuals redirect their personal vision and empower themselves, an entire pattern may begin to change. And so it is now with the nursing profession. Most of use conceptualize nursing as much more than a vocation. We are greater than our individual roles as scientists, specialists, or care deliverers. We currently search for a name to put on our new conception of the empowered nurse. The recently introduced term *nurse-healer* aptly describes the qualities of an increasing number of clinicians, educators, administrators, and nurse practitioners. Today all nurses are awakening to the realization that they have the potential for healing.

It is my feeling that most nurses, when awakened and guided to develop their own healing potential, will function both as nurses and healers. Thus, the concept of nurse as healer is born. When nurses realize they have the ability to evoke others' healing, as well as care for them, a shift of consciousness begins to occur. As individual awareness and changes in skill building occur, a collective under-standing of this new concept emerges. This knowledge, along with a shift in attitudes and new kinds of behavior, allows empowered nurses to renew themselves in an expanded role. The Nurse As Healer Series is born out of the belief that nurses are ready to embrace guidance that inspires them in their journeys of empowerment. Each book in the series may stand alone or be used in complementary fashion with other books. I hope and believe that information herein will strengthen you both personally and professionally, and provide you with the help and confidence to embark upon the path of nurse-healer.

Titles in the Nurse As Healer Series:

Healing Touch: A Resource for Health Care Professionals

Healing Life's Crises: A Guide for Nurses

The Nurse's Meditative Journal

Healing Nutrition

Healing the Dying

Awareness in Healing

Creative Imagery in Nursing

CONTENTS

Foreword, xi
Preface, xii
Introduction: Knowing the Self, xiv

Part 1   MEDITATION, 1

Chapter 1   The Nature of Meditation, 3
What is Meditation?, 3
   States of Consciousness, 3

An Ancient Tradition, 4

Why Meditate?, 5
   Benefits of Meditation, 5

Gurus and Other Teachers, 6
   Choosing an Instructor, 7

The Goal of Meditation, 7

References, 8

Chapter 2   Physiological Benefits of Meditation, 11
Bodymind, 11

Physiological Findings, 12
   Early Research, 12
   Recent Findings, 13

Meditation and Longevity, 14

References, 16

Chapter 3   ***Psychological and Other Benefits of Meditation, 19***

Changing the Psyche, 19

Psychological Findings, 19
  Early Research, 19
  Recent Research, 21

Meditation as Psychotherapy, 21

Meditation, Productivity, and Creativity, 23
  Increased Productivity, 23
  Enhanced Creativity, 23

References, 24

Chapter 4   ***Types of Meditative Practice, 27***

A Variety from which to Choose, 27

Concentration, 27
  Candle Flame, 28
  Breath, 28
  Mantra, 28

Contemplation, 28

Devotion, 29

Mindfulness, 29

Movement, 29
  Hatha Yoga, 30
  T'ai Chi, 30
  Sufi Dancing, 30

Selecting Your Path, 30

Chapter 5   ***Preparing for Meditation, 33***

Cornerstones of Meditation, 33
  Relaxation, 33
  Concentration, 35

General Guidelines for Meditation, 36
  Creating Your Sacred Space, 37
  Establishing a Routine, 37
  Body Positioning, 38

Chapter 6   ***Meditative Techniques, 39***

The How of What You Do, 39

A Variety of Techniques, 40
  Thought Watching, 40

Breath, 41
  The Power of the Breath, 41

Diaphragmatic Breathing, 41
Breath Meditation, 42

Mantra, 43
Preparing for Mantra Meditation, 43
Mantra Meditation, 44

Contemplation, 45
Contemplative Nature Meditation, 45
Contemplative Reading Meditation, 46

Mindfulness, 46
Thought-Watching Mindfulness Meditation, 47
Eating Mindfulness Meditation, 47

References, 48

Chapter 7   **Moving Deeper, 51**

Internal Tools, 51
Deep Breathing, 51
Auming, 52
Twirling, 52
Music, 53
Thought Specifying, 53
Meditative Visualization, 54

Sacred Places, 54

Group Meditation, 54

Portable Peace, 55

Chapter 8   **Experiences Along the Way, 57**

A Time for Every Purpose Under Heaven, 57

Ruts, 57

Bumps, 58
Surfacing the Subconscious, 58
Updating Your Reality, 59
The Releasing Process, 59
Tools and Guides to Assist You, 60

Spectacles, 61

Part 2   JOURNAL WRITING, 63

Chapter 9   **Writing for Yourself, 65**

Your Childhood Diary, 65

Your Adult Journal, 65

The Process of Writing, 66
Letting It Flow, 66
Meditation Helps You Write, 66

Preparing for a Journal Writing Session, 67

Reference, 67

Chapter 10 Journal Writing Focuses, 69

Looking Within, 69

Selecting Focuses, 70
  Recording Observations, Insights, and
  Revelations, 70
  Contemplative Focus, 72
  Meditative Material, 72
  Dreams, 73

Chapter 11 Journal Writing Techniques, 75

Connecting the Inner and Outer, 75

Quieting Unwanted Voices, 75
  Putting the Critic to Sleep, 75
  Setting the Editor Aside, 76

Flow Writing, 76

Writing with Your Nondominant Hand, 77

Dialogue, 78

Mindmapping, 79

References, 82

Chapter 12 Release and Renewal, 83

Powerful Tools, 83

Journal Writing Surfaced Material, 83

Working with Forgiveness, 84
  Journal Writing for Release, 85
  Affirmative Meditation for Release, 86

Creating Your Own Way, 86

Part 3   **PERSONAL JOURNAL PAGES, 87**

F O R E W O R D

Consider this book a gift to yourself. It is a perfect companion and guide for you as your move along your journey of self- and professional discovery. Personal mastery has been identified as one of the key elements for professional success in the twenty-first century[1]. Knowing yourself is part of this personal mastery. In *The Nurse's Meditative Journal,* Sherry Kahn provides you with techniques and methods for spiritual fitness and personal development. I have enjoyed learning more about this dimension of myself and believe it will enhance my effectiveness as a care provider.

This book is a good complement to Sherry's first book for nurses, *Healing Yourself: A Nurse's Guide to Self-Care and Renewal*[2]. It is organized so that you can read one short chapter at a time, but I found myself not wanting to put it down until I could get started with the meditative exercises and journal writing. It's easy to read and easy to understand.

I believe that nurses hold the key to providing holistic care in the next century. Our current health care system is maximally challenged to be relevant to its customers, our patients. By tuning in to ourselves and to the spirituality of our patients, we can be better advocates for meeting their needs. This book is a tool to help you do just that.

Jan Boller, RN, MSN
Doctoral Student, UCSF School of Nursing
Former Program Development Director
American Association of Critical-Care Nurses

---

[1] Senge, P. M. (1990). *The fifth discipline: The art and practice of the learning organization.* New York: Doubleday.

[2] Kahn, S., & Saulo, M. (1994). *Healing yourself: A nurse's guide to self-care and renewal.* Albany, NY: Delmar Publishers Inc.

P R E F A C E

Who you are as a nursing professional is as important, if not more so, as what you do. Doing what you do well makes you a competent caregiver. But being who you are, expressing your true nature, can transform you from a capable provider into a healing presence.

Your presence — your ability to be a focal point of peace in an environment of chaos, love in an atmosphere of conflict, understanding and clarity in the midst of confusion — definitely makes a difference. Your expression of these qualities brings comfort to your patients and can inspire your coworkers to find these same qualities within themselves. And because who you are is who you are 24 hours a day, those in your personal orbit — family, significant others, and friends — are similarly benefited.

These wonderful qualities are not limited to just a few; they are actually the true nature of all. Unfortunately, they are frequently clouded by childhood experiences and cultural conditioning. With the right tools, however, the clouds can be dispersed to reveal the compassionate, vital, creative person you really are. *The Nurse's Meditative Journal* provides you with two such tools — meditation and journal writing — for reaching into those deep personal spaces and reclaiming your true self.

Meditation, as has been well documented in the scientific literature, decreases stress and enhances both physiological and psychological functioning. New evidence shows that meditation can not only improve the quality of your life but actually increase its duration. But even more than this, it provides you with a new perspective — a way of seeing the world in a holistic rather than mechanistic way — a capability that is so very important in these rapidly changing and uncertain times. Journal writing is a way to integrate your inner and outer worlds, a means for understanding more about who you really are and for releasing outdated concepts.

These two tools for self-exploration and growth are intricately interlinked. Journal writing allows you to chart the changing you as you unfold and grow through meditation, and meditation provides content for journal writing. Together they are two valuable friends who can guide and assist you in your journey. Here, in one book, you are provided with detailed instruction on both meditation and journal writing, and a year-long grouping of blank journal pages are included for your personal use.

This book, itself, is a demonstration of the wonderful benefits of meditation for both the concept and form, as with the earlier Delmar publication *Healing Yourself: A Nurse's Guide to Self-Care and Renewal*, came to me in the silence within my inner sanctuary. And the writing of it has been a most rewarding part of my personal journey.

My deepest and heartfelt gratitude is expressed to my spiritual teachers, both visible and invisible, without whom this book could not have been written. Once again, I thank William Burgower, senior administrative editor at Delmar, for his receptivity and willingness to explore new territory. And special thanks go to Lorena Bennett and Jan Boller for their interest and input.

RESOURCES

For information regarding continuing education workshops, retreats, and materials for renewal and transformation, please contact:

Sherry Kahn, MPH
Self-Care for Caregivers
(310) 285-3245

INTRODUCTION:
KNOWING THE SELF

In seeking myself I find who I am.

Most of us were raised to survive in the world. We went to school and were taught how to read and write and do arithmetic. These were the building blocks, the foundation for additional academic subjects. Most of us were also brought up within some sort of religious or ethical framework. This may have been formalized by attendance of religious services or classes, or it may have been less formal, with parents instilling within us the moral beliefs of our culture by their example and/or their instruction. Later came nursing school where we absorbed both the technical skills and the ethical culture of the profession.

Now, you are a working nurse with both professional and personal responsibilities. Your career can be stressful at times as you are constantly in a nurturing mode, and given the financial constraints of the current health care environment, you may find yourself working under less than ideal conditions. Home may be a place of comfort, or it may provide you with yet another opportunity to test your coping skills.

You may be one of those individuals who is a planner — competent, efficient, and upbeat. But what happens when things do not play out as you planned them? Do you adapt easily to the changes, or do you find yourself creating another plan to control what just happened? Or are you a person who always appears to be moving in fast motion, but somehow does not really get anything accomplished, and your life is always on the edge of chaos?

Are you one of those people who is happy when things (or most things) are going your way but who falls apart when your external circumstances change? Do you use food, drugs, alcohol, or sex to anesthetize yourself from the pain of your disappointments? Or are you a person who usually promises more than you can deliver and then feels guilty about not being able to fulfill those promises?

Are you someone who was very creative as a child — you loved to dance or sing or paint or write stories — but you do not do that anymore because you have "a real job" and other adult responsibilities? Or perhaps you know deep inside that you are capable of doing a lot more with your life than you currently are but are afraid of moving forward.

What happened to you and just about everyone else is that you became very busy with the business of living. And in that "busyness" you lost track of those moments of peace, stillness, harmony, and pure joy you probably experienced at one time or another as a child. In adapting to survival in the world that the mass culture collectively calls "real," you lost your true self — not the small self who is the nurse, sister, mother, wife, or lover, but the bigger self who is part of and one with everything and everyone in the universe.

Although you learned ways of surviving in the day-to-day world, using your technical nursing skills and the ethical framework within which to live both your professional and personal lives, you were not given tools for living and knowing your true self.

Tools for living are those that you can use to become more competent and serene, to stay centered in the midst of disruption, be compassionate toward those who have wronged you, see clearly what the reality of the situation is, deeply understand people, release or develop creativity, and discover your true nature. Meditation and journal writing are two such tools for living.

Part 1 of this book deals with meditation. Chapter 1 describes the nature of meditation. Chapters 2 and 3 offer scientific evidence for the physiological and psychological benefits of meditative practice for those interested in research specifics. Part 1 then moves on to provide you with an overview of a variety of meditative techniques.

With this background established, you are then provided with step-by-step instructions for four different styles of meditation. Later chapters describe how to integrate meditation into your daily life and guide you through common experiences on your meditative journey.

Part 2 of the book focuses on journal writing, which has two primary purposes — monitoring growth and self-exploration. The beginning chapters of this section define journal writing, its goals, and potential focuses. Specific instructions on the use of a variety of writing techniques are presented. This part concludes with a chapter describing specific ways in which you can combine your meditative and journal writing practices.

Part 3 is a blank, personal journal divided into 52 weeks. Each two-page weekly spread contains a brief spiritual statement designed for one style of meditation — contemplation. The pages may be used to write a response to the statements or in a variety of other ways, which are described in part 2.

Even though you are adult, you never stop growing unless you so choose. This book gives you some tools with which to grow and to live. Your journal pages are blank. Create something new and wonderful for yourself this year, and by all means, enjoy the process.

1 | MEDITATION

In the peace of the silence I experience what it is to be truly alive.

1 | THE NATURE OF MEDITATION

Be still and know.

WHAT IS MEDITATION?

Meditation is a state of consciousness, an experience of mind. It is not a withdrawing from the world but rather a way of being more fully in the world in the present moment.

States of Consciousness

Most of us are aware of varying states of consciousness that we experience daily. Our waking time is a time of active mind — thinking, planning, doing. Then there is our sleeping time, that time when our conscious mind moves into what appears to be a state of forgetfulness. The middle stage of consciousness, of which we are sometimes aware, is the dream state. At times we bring back what we experienced in our dreams to our wakeful, active mind, whereas at others we remember experiencing that state of consciousness but have no memory of the content.

There is, however, a fourth state of consciousness called *pure awareness.* Meditation is this state of consciousness. It is a moving of the mind from a state of activity into a state of silence and being in that silence in a relaxed and alert manner. A feeling is also associated with this state — a feeling of oneness, of unity, of a connection with something far greater than your individual self.

Everyone has had this feeling at one time or another. It may have come during a sunset on the beach as you watched and listened to the continuous, rhythmic breaking of the waves on the shore. Perhaps you experienced it while observing the first snowflakes of the season fall and drift to settle softly on the needles of the pine tree outside your bedroom window. You may have had such a moment connecting deeply through eye contact with a patient. That moment of sexual ecstasy with a loved one may have moved you to that feeling of one-ness, or maybe it was the smile of a newborn baby that opened such a space for you.

Somewhere, sometime, and hopefully more than once, you have experienced uniting with something far more than yourself. That some-thing you may call God, humanhood, Spirit, the universe, the unified field. It matters not what you call it, but that you know it. Meditation simply allows you to experience that state of consciousness, of being-ness, whenever you so desire. And with continued practice, it allows you to experience that state of awareness in your everyday life.

AN ANCIENT TRADITION

Meditation was introduced in the United States when tie-dye T-shirts and bell bottoms were the costume of the day. The Beatles were at the top of the pop music charts, and the Maharishi brought transcen-dental meditation (TM) to the streets of America. Previously confined to monasteries and ashrams, meditation teaching became accessible to anyone living in a major city. The last 30 years have seen the coming (and going) of many Eastern and Western meditative teachings and teachers.

Although relatively new in the United States, meditative practices are ancient. The teaching and practice of meditation originated in India. Early teachings have been traced to Syria and Jordan in the 5th to 12th centuries and to Japan in the 10th century. Meditation was also a routine practice in Christian medieval monasteries. Every religious tradition incorporates meditation into its practices, but you do not need to be religious or participate in religious services to practice and ben-efit from meditation.

The beauty of meditation is that, once learned, it can be practiced anywhere at any time. And there are many forms — sitting, moving, chanting — so there is no need to make yourself fit the method. You can choose the form or forms that are best for you.

WHY MEDITATE?

Many people are drawn to meditation not because they want to experience a state of consciousness or commune with God, but because they are in pain or are suffering and want a way out. Others simply have an uneasy sense that there must be something more to living than what they are currently experiencing.

Low self-esteem, anxiety, frustration, feelings of isolation, fear, nervousness, anger, and unsatisfying relationships or work are some of the common conditions that push people toward meditation. Although these conditions appear diverse, the underlying commonality among them all is a feeling of separation from life. When drugs, alcohol, eating, compulsive sex, and relationships do not relieve the pain, the angst, the isolation, an opening is created to try something new. That something is often meditation.

Benefits of Meditation

Meditators do experience less anxiety and more peace than nonmeditators. Meditation is an effective stress reduction tool with both physiological and psychological benefits, but it is more than this. It is about more than getting rid of the "bad stuff" in your life; it is about merging with the "good stuff," with universal peace, harmony, beauty, wisdom, and creativity. And in the acceptance of the good, you shift to a new worldview, a new understanding of reality.

This understanding perceives the universe as timeless and eternal. You are not merely the small self encased in your body but are an individualized expression of eternal life. Albert Einstein wrote of this state of being in a letter to a friend: "I feel myself so much a part of all life that I am not in the least concerned with the beginning or the end of the concrete existence of any particular person in this unending stream" (Chopra, 1993).

As you begin to know and live that worldview as a result of your meditative practice, you become more peaceful, more loving, and happier. You begin to understand that thoughts and conditions are temporary appearances, not who you are. For example, a rainbow is a transient appearance created by temporary conditions of light and humidity. The rainbow is here one moment and gone the next. But the ultimate cause of that rainbow, the eternal life that has no beginning or ending, is the true nature of reality.

With this understanding, you become detached from the comings and goings of the world; the people, events, and circumstances that once snagged you, and to which you reacted, no longer have a hold on you. This is what is meant by the saying, "Be in the world but not of it."

As you become quieter and your perceptions become clearer, you create a more positive atmosphere for yourself. You will notice that what you experience in the world around you also changes as you change, for like attracts like. You feel and live this oneness and become a radiant presence to your patients, your coworkers, and your loved ones.

GURUS AND OTHER TEACHERS

The meditation techniques presented in chapter 6 do not require a teacher. You can start to meditate right now on your own. This book also includes instruction on how to deepen your practice, how to move through dry periods and resistance, and how to deal with personal issues that may arise as a result of your meditative practice in the course of your unfoldment.

Some people, however, find it useful to take meditation classes or to have a meditation teacher. Some are comfortable with one teacher, and others benefit from the instruction of a variety of teachers and traditions. If you are having trouble disciplining yourself to practice, a structured setting can be helpful. Another advantage of participating in group classes or retreats is the sense of community experienced in these environments. A teacher may also serve as a mentor and guide, assisting you in your spiritual unfoldment and easing your passage through the rough spots.

Many varieties of gurus and meditation teachers are available. The teacher who is right for you may not be right for your friend and vice versa. Just as the method of practice you select is highly individualized, so is a meditation teacher.

In the Hindu tradition, if you want to pursue spiritual practice you become a disciple of a guru (a spiritual teacher, mentor, and guide). The intent of this relationship is for you to surrender the ego — that set of thoughts that define your universe — to the larger awareness of the universe as embodied in the form of the guru. The disciple often lives in an ashram, a sequestered community, with the chosen guru. Both the Christian and Buddhist traditions offer monasteries where aspirants can withdraw from everyday life, and in the company of fellow seekers engage in their chosen study with the teachers in the monastery.

In our modern world there has been a trend to combine the secular and the spiritual lives. Although a few do go off to ashrams and monasteries, more often people are bringing their spiritual practices into everyday life. The journey then is not about withdrawing from your daily responsibilities but rather bringing heaven to earth and living as a spiritual being in a material world. Because this is the choice of many today, a variety of meditation teachers offer classes that you can participate in on a regular basis while you continue with your daily routine.

Choosing an Instructor

If you do feel a need for a personal instructor and mentor, it is important to ask yourself some questions about each teacher you are considering. First, "Does the teacher walk the talk or only talk the talk?" During the past decade or so, some well-known gurus and spiritual teachers were exposed for not practicing what they preached, and some were accused of a variety of illegal activities. So it is important to ask, "How does this person live his or her life?"

A question closely associated with the above question is, "Does this teaching have an ethical basis?" For example, Christian/Judaic traditions are based upon the Ten Commandments, whereas the ethical basis of Buddhist teachings is the Noble Eightfold Path. Some meditation teachers are more interested in teaching their students how to develop extrasensory powers than in how to live spiritually. Although these abilities do sometimes develop as a side effect of meditation, the development of such is not the goal of spiritual practice.

The next question to ask is, "Does this teacher create a dependency on him or her?" Because knowing the self can only be known by the self, the teaching you select should give you the tools to do so. True spiritual teachings are those that give you back to you. They foster self-responsibility, not dependency on any person or dogma.

THE GOAL OF MEDITATION

Many talk about the ultimate goal of meditation being enlightenment — that level of awareness where you are in a constant state of oneness with the unbounded universe. What is more important, however, is to discover the awareness and presence that is possible here and now. The daily goal of meditation is to be absolutely open with your heart and mind to the interconnectedness of all life and to experience that fully.

Buddhist teacher Jack Kornfield, when recently queried about meditation in an interview about his new book *A Path With Heart,* responded, "Meditation is most fundamentally a training for living well and dying well, a training for compassion and understanding that can allow you to be wise in the midst of all changing experiences" (Kenaston, 1993).

It is important to ask the right questions about the results of meditation. The question is not, "Am I enlightened?" The more appropriate questions to ask yourself in comparing the difference between your premeditative self and your meditative self are: "Am I more compassionate and loving?" "Am I less judgmental?" "Do I feel more unified with everything and everyone around me?" "Am I more forgiving?" "Am I more flexible?" "Is my happiness less affected by external events?"

If you answer "yes" to those questions, you know that you are progressing well on the meditator's journey. If your "yes's" are mixed with "no's," it simply means you need to do one thing — meditate more.

References

Chopra, D. (1993). *Ageless body, timeless mind.* New York: Crown Publishers, Inc.

Kenaston, M. (1993, Winter). A path with heart. *Bodhi Tree Bookstore Quarterly,* Issue No. 7. Los Angeles: Bodhi Tree Bookstore.

Suggested Reading

Addington, J., & Addington, C. (1990). *The joy of meditation* (6th ed.). Marina del Rey, CA: DeVorss.

Chinmoy, Sr. (1984). *Meditation: Man-perfection in God-satisfaction* (5th ed.). Jamaica, NY: Agni Press.

Goldsmith, J. (1990). *The art of meditation.* New York: HarperCollins.

Hanh, Thich Nhat. (1987). *Being peace.* Berkeley, CA: Parallax Press.

Kornfield, J. (1993). *A path with heart.* New York: Bantam.

Krishnamurti. (1964). *Think on these things.* New York: Harper & Row Publishers, Inc.

Larson, C. (1993). *The pathway of roses.* Lakewood, CA: Mannahouse Publishing.

Thurman, H. (1984). *For the inward journey.* Richmond, IN: Friends United Meeting.

Yogananda, P. (1975). *Man's eternal quest.* Los Angeles: Self-Realization Fellowship.

2 | PHYSIOLOGICAL BENEFITS OF MEDITATION

In the silence of the mind the body, too, becomes peaceful.

BODYMIND

Being aware of the *bodymind* feedback system provides a foundation for understanding how meditation can influence physiological functions. The bodymind concept has grown out of the findings of psychoneuroimmunology (PNI) — the study of the interrelationships among the mind (psychology), the brain (neurology), and the body's natural healing system (immunology).

PNI research has shown that three communications systems — the central nervous system (CNS), the autonomic nervous system (ANS), and the neuropeptide chemical messenger system — are inextricably linked in a continuous feedback loop. What was previously thought to be separate, the body and the mind, is actually one: the bodymind. The mind thinks and sends messages to the body, and every cell in the body thinks and sends messages back to the mind.

Neuropeptides (such as endorphins) have been shown to increase in response to positive feelings and thoughts and to decrease their synthesis in response to negative feelings and thoughts. Dr. Deepak Chopra (1990), an endocrinologist and one of the foremost pioneers in PNI, illustrates this concept with the story of the progress of a terminal cancer patient. The patient, apparently on the verge of dying, was given an experimental drug. His positive response to the medication was dramatic, resulting in a sharp decrease of his tumors. However, after reading a news report discrediting the treatment, the patient went into severe relapse. He then rebounded when given a double dose of the drug, only to fall into a depression after another news account of its worthlessness; he died soon thereafter (Chopra, 1990).

PHYSIOLOGICAL FINDINGS

Meditation has been found to increase feelings of harmony, peacefulness, and happiness and decrease worry, anxiety, anger, and hostility. Scientific research over the past two decades has confirmed the positive influence of these states of mind on the physical body.

The first research study of the physiological effects of meditation in the United States was a 1970 doctoral research dissertation at UCLA. Recent years have seen a proliferation of interest and research in this area, with more than 60 studies published internationally in medical journals in the last 3 years alone.

Early Research

Physiologist Dr. R. Keith Wallace (1970) monitored a number of body functions of college-age students as they sat in meditation. This pioneering study, along with subsequent ones with cardiologist Dr. Herbert Benson (1971), found that meditators showed significantly decreased blood pressures, cardiac output, and levels of oxygen consumption during the period of their meditation. The drop in oxygen consumption was particularly interesting because the amount of decrease was greater than that experienced during sleep. Finding that the respiratory quotient did not change, the researchers concluded that the metabolic rate of the body was also lower during meditation. Meditation was, thus, a state of hypometabolic wakefulness — metabolism decreased but wakeful consciousness was retained.

Other early studies revealed that blood lactate levels, associated with states of anxiety and tension, were substantially lower in meditation than during comparable periods of quiet rest (Wallace, Benson, Wilson, & Garrett, 1971). Studies of meditators in Germany found that during meditation there was a simultaneous increase in peripheral blood flow and decrease in both heart rate and cardiac output. Researchers concluded that the heart is able to deliver more blood to the musculature with less effort during meditation (Reichart, 1967).

Dr. David Orme-Johnson (1973), using galvanic skin response as a measure of relaxation, found in his study that meditators in comparison to nonmeditators have increased stability of the autonomic nervous system and improved adaptability and resistance to stress.

Significant differences have been found between meditators and nonmeditators in research studies in terms of cerebral cortical activity, alpha and theta brain waves, and synchronicity of left and right and front and back brain waves. The implications of these findings will be discussed in the context of psychological and other effects of meditation in chapter 3.

Recent Findings

Recent research has confirmed the findings of these pioneering studies. A study by Dr. Wallace and two associates found meditation to be an integrated response, with peripheral circulatory and metabolic changes subserving increased central nervous activity. Physiological findings during meditation included increased cerebral blood flow, cessation of CO_2 generation by muscles, ECG synchrony, and a fivefold plasma AVP elevation. The researchers concluded that meditation is a very relaxed but, at the same time, a very alert state (Jeuning, Wallace, & Beidebach, 1992).

A recent study of physiological measures of Buddhist meditators after meditation found that in comparison to nonmeditators the meditators had decreased serum cortisol, serum protein, systolic and diastolic pressures, pulse rate, reaction time, vital capacity, tidal volume, and maximal voluntary ventilation (Sudsuang, Chentanez, & Veluvan, 1991).

A study of regional brain glucose metabolism found the brain to exhibit holistic metabolic behavior during the meditative state (Herzog et al., 1990–1991). Another study found meditation to be associated with reduced sympathetic adrenergic receptor sensitivity (Mills, Schneider, Hill, Walton, & Wallace, 1990).

A recent medical journal report focused on the effectiveness of meditation in relieving the painful symptoms of patients with fibromyalgia (Kaplan, Goldberg, & Galvin-Nadenin, 1993). More evidence regarding the effectiveness of meditation in relieving pain was presented in the Public Broadcasting Service television special *Healing and the Mind* (1993) in its segment on the work being done at the University of Massachusetts Stress Clinic. More than 5,000 patients with a variety of extreme pain-producing conditions have participated in the meditation program offered through this clinic. The regular practice of meditation has offered relief from pain for 75% of the participants, and 90% of the patients are still meditating 4 years after completing the course.

Meditation has also been shown to have a positive effect on the functioning of the immune system. Studies of meditative training by immunologist Dr. Ronald Glaser and psychologist Dr. Janice-Kiecolt-Glaser (1985, 1986) found increased NK- and T-cell activity as a result of the practice of meditation. Associated findings were recently described by Dr. Joan Borysenko in her book *A New Psychology of Spiritual Optimism* (1993). She reports a doubling in NK-cell activity in people who have a sense of connectedness relative to people who feel isolated and lonely.

MEDITATION AND LONGEVITY

Perhaps the most exciting new research findings are those regarding the physiological effects of meditation on longevity, described by Dr. Chopra in his book *Ageless Body, Timeless Mind* (Chopra, 1993).

According to Chopra, Dr. Wallace initiated the study of the effects of meditation on human aging in 1978 using measures of blood pressure, hearing threshold, and near vision, all of which typically are less functional in older adults. Each of these functions improved with the long-term practice of meditation. Study subjects who had been meditating for fewer than 5 years were, on the average, biologically 5 years younger than their chronological ages; those who had been meditating for greater than 5 years, were, on the average, 12 years younger than their chronological ages. These results were consistent for both older and younger subjects, and were dramatic indications of the actual reversal of aging through the practice of meditation.

Later research, examining the health status of 2,000 meditators in a group insurance plan, proved equally significant. In relation to the control group of nonmeditators, the meditators had only half as many physician visits and hospitalizations. In 13 major disease categories, the meditators were significantly healthier. This group showed dramatic differences in relation to their nonmeditating peers in the two leading killer diseases — cancer and heart disease. The meditating group had more than 50% less cancer and 80% less heart disease. Perhaps most significant was the finding that meditators 65 years and older showed the most improvement.

Recent research conducted by Dr. Jay Glaser, Chopra, and associates has provided additional evidence regarding the relationship of meditation to aging (Glaser et al., 1992). This study focused on dehydroepiandosterone (DHEA), a steroid secreted by the adrenal cortex. Although the precise function of DHEA in the body is still unknown, it is the only hormone that shows a linear decline with age, peaking around age 25 and decreasing to approximately 5% of that level by the last year of life. It is also known that DHEA is a precursor of the stress hormones adrenaline and cortisol. Thus, every time the body exhibits a stress response it has a little less DHEA.

Higher DHEA levels are associated with decreased death from all diseases and longer survival in older men. In individuals with higher DHEA levels, there is less incidence of coronary artery disease, osteoporosis, and breast cancer. Alzheimer patients have been found to have approximately half the level of DHEA relative to age-matched controls.

The Glaser study compared the DHEA levels of 328 seasoned meditators with 1,462 nonmeditating controls and included men and women and a broad range of ages. Findings showed the meditators' DHEA levels to be equivalent to those of individuals 5 to 10 years younger. The largest differences occurred in subjects over the age of 45, with meditating women having 47% more and meditating men 23% more DHEA than their nonmeditating age-matched peers. And, quite significantly, these results were independent of other possible contributing factors such as exercise, diet, weight, and alcohol consumption.

The mechanics of this finding are interesting to ponder. Meditation is a state of hypometabolic wakefulness. In this state the body experiences deep rest. This is a stressless state as well as a timeless state. If the mind is solely in the present moment, there is no memory of past events, feelings, or thoughts that may have been stressful; nor is there anticipation or fear of potential stress. There is only the present moment of silence and peace.

The body exists in this stressless state during the time of meditation. An experienced meditator typically spends 40 to 60 minutes or more each day in this state of consciousness. During this time the body experiences no stress, and no DHEA is required to produce stress hormones. The effects of meditation are also cumulative, for the mind and body over time begin to remember the meditative state and carry this consciousness into the everyday world. There is an increased sense of peacefulness and detachment, and subsequently fewer stress reactions such as fear, anger, anxiety, and nervousness, and less release of DHEA. The understanding that good health and increased longevity can be achieved solely by a state of awareness has very exciting implications for the future of the human species.

References

Borysenko, J. (1993). *Fire in the soul: A new psychology of spiritual optimism.* New York: Warner Books.

Chopra, D. (1990). *Quantum healing: Exploring the frontiers of mind/body medicine.* New York: Bantam Books.

Chopra, D. (1993). *Ageless body, timeless mind.* New York: Crown Publishers, Inc.

Glaser, J. L., Brind, J. L., Vogelman, J. H., Eisner, M. J., Dillbeck, M. C., Wallace, R. K., Chopra, D., & Orentreich, N. (1992, August 15). Elevated serum dehydroepiandosterone sulfate levels in practitioners of the transcendental meditation (TM) and TM-Sidhi programs. *Journal of Behavioral Medicine, 4,* 327–341.

Herzog, H., Lele, V. R., Kuwert, T., Langen, K. J., Kops, E. R., & Feindegen, L. E. (1990–1991). Changed pattern of regional glucose metabolism during yoga meditative relaxation. *Neuropsychobiology, 23*(4), 182–187.

Jeuning, R., Wallace, R. K., & Beidebach, M. (1992, Fall). The physiology of meditation: A review. A wakeful hypometabolic integrated response. *Neuroscience and Biobehavioral Reviews, 16*(3), 415–424.

Kaplan, K. H., Goldberg, D. L., & Galvin-Nadenin, M. (1993, September). The impact of meditation-based stress reduction program on fibromyalgia. *General Hospital Psychiatry, 15*(5), 284–289.

Kiecolt-Glaser, J. K., Glaser, R., Strain, E. C., Stout, J. C., Tarr, K. L., Holliday, J. E., & Speicher, C. E. (1986). Modulation of cellular immunity in medical students. *Journal of Behavioral Medicine, 9,* 5–21.

Kiecolt-Glaser, J. K., Glaser, R., Williger, D., Stout, J., Messick, G., Sheppard, S., Ricker, D., Romisher, S. C., Briner, W., & Bonnell, G. (1985). Psychosocial enhancement of immunocompetence in a geriatric population. *Health Psychology, 4,* 24–41.

Mills, P. J., Schneider, R. H., Hill, D., Walton, K. G., & Wallace, R. K. (1990). Beta-adrenergic receptor sensitivity in subjects practicing transcendental meditation. *Journal of Psychosomatic Research, 34*(1), 29–33.

Orme-Johnson, D. (1973, July–August). Autonomic stability and transcendental meditation. *Psychosomatic Medicine, 35*(4), 341–349.

Reichart, H. (1967). Plethsmographische untersuchungen bei konsentrations and meditations ubugen arlich forsche. *Artliche Forsch, 21,* 61–65.

Sudsuang, R., Chentanez, V., & Veluvan, K. (1991, September). Effect of Buddhist meditation on serum cortisol and total protein levels, blood pressure, pulse rate, lung volume, and reaction time. *Physiology and Behavior, 50*(3), 543–548.

Wallace, R. K. (1970, March 27). Physiolgical effects of transcendental meditation. *Science, 167,* 1751–1754.

Wallace, R. K., Benson, H., & Wilson, A. F. (1971, September). A wakeful hypometabolic physiologic state. *American Journal of Physiology, 221*(3) 759–799.

Wallace, R. K., Benson, H., Wilson, A., & Garrett, M. (1971, March–April). Decreased blood lactate during transcendental meditation. *Proceedings of the Federation of American Society for Experimental Biology, 30*(2), 376.

WNET. (1993). Healing and the mind [video]. New York: Public Broadcasting Service.

PSYCHOLOGICAL AND OTHER BENEFITS OF MEDITATION

Anything unlike peace and harmony simply falls away.

CHANGING THE PSYCHE

In addition to beneficial physiological changes, the practice of meditation has a dramatic impact on psychological well-being, including response to stress, emotional stability, self-concept, and social interaction, as well as in the associated areas of productivity, creativity, and the actualization of talent potentials. Meditators typically report decreased anxiety, fewer episodes of anger and hostility, and lessened dependence on external stimuli such as drugs or excitement for self-mobilization. They also note that they are happier, more stable, optimistic, energetic, and experience enhanced productivity and performance.

PSYCHOLOGICAL FINDINGS

Early Research

In the early 1970s, psychologist Maynard Shelly (1972) undertook a study comparing meditators and nonmeditators on measures of psychological well-being. The meditating group was more relaxed, happier, and less sad. They experienced joy more frequently, developed deeper personal relationships, and depended less on their external circumstances for happiness. Shelly also noted that the meditators showed more development of resources for achieving their personal goals as well as a greater ability to mobilize those resources.

A study conducted at the University of Cincinnati found that the meditators relative to the nonmeditators showed increased spontaneity, self-regard, capacity for intimate contact, and acceptance of aggression (Nidich, Seeman, & Dreskin, 1974). This study confirmed earlier results reported by L. Hjelle (1972). Still other studies have shown meditation to decrease neuroticism, manifest anxiety, hypochondria, personality disorder, nervousness, depression, irritability, hostility, tendency to dominate, and inhibition (Boese & Berger, 1972; Fehr, Nerstherimer, & Torber, 1974; Orme-Johnson, 1974).

Dr. Herbert Benson (1969) was the first to report the effect of meditation on drug abuse when he noted that all but one of the meditators in his study had given up the use of drugs. A larger follow-up study confirmed Benson's report, finding that 84% of those who had been meditating for at least 3 months and had been regular marijuana users prior to taking up meditation had stopped, and that another 14% had decreased their use (Winquist, 1969). Similar results were observed in this same study in individuals who had been regular users of psychedelic drugs, with 86% stopping and 14% decreasing use after learning how to meditate. Later studies found similar results for not only marijuana and LSD but also barbiturates, amphetamines, narcotics, alcohol, and cigarettes (Benson & Wallace, 1972). These dramatic findings have been replicated in a number of other studies.

Contrary to common belief, meditators report increased rather than decreased activity and improved performance in all areas of endeavor. Because performance is tied to perceptual ability, psychologist Kenneth Pelletier (1972) performed a comparative study of meditator and nonmeditator perceptual ability. The meditators performed better than the nonmeditating group on the perceptual tasks, leading Pelletier to conclude that the meditators had both a greater ability to concentrate and a greater resistance to distraction. Other perceptual ability studies that looked at auditory and visual discrimination found that meditators consistently showed increased abilities in relation to nonmeditators (Brown, Stewart, & Blodgett, 1972; Graham, 1974).

Hand-eye coordination, an ability directly linked to performance, was another area of early scientific inquiry into the effects of meditation. Meditators showed much greater perceptual-motor coordination than nonmeditators, completing the tasks both more accurately and quicker than the control group (Blasdell, 1974). Other subsequent studies showed similar results on perceptual-motor coordination tasks.

Yet another study found that meditators demonstrated increased learning capabilities compared to nonmeditators on recall tasks, and that those who had been meditating longer performed better than those who had been practicing for a shorter time. These initial results led to the speculation that the impact of meditation has cumulative effects (Abrams, 1974).

Recent Research

Findings of more recent studies have been consistent with earlier ones. A recent study of a Buddhist mindfulness meditation program found that the program reduced symptoms of anxiety and panic and helped maintain these reductions in patients with panic disorder, panic disorder with agoraphobia, and generalized anxiety disorder (Kabat-Zinn et al., 1992).

Research conducted in Taiwan found that nurses who participated in relaxation training involving visualization and meditation reported significantly lowered stress levels and significantly increased levels of psychophysiologic health than a control group who spent comparable time listening to theoretical lectures (Tsai & Crockett, 1993).

A study of long-term meditators concluded that psychological health can be developed through systematic practice of meditation (Gelderloss, Hermans, Ahlserom, & Jacoby, 1990). Another study of long-term meditators found that those who had been meditating for more than 6 years showed the most psychologically healthy profile, and that participation in a meditative retreat of either 2 weeks or 3 months had the largest and most positive effect on the psychological profile (Shapiro, 1992).

MEDITATION AS PSYCHOTHERAPY

These studies provide scientific evidence that meditation does create positive psychological changes, ranging from decreases in substance abuse and anxiety to improved self-esteem and social interaction. It is understandable from the physiological evidence that the body is more relaxed. This explains why meditators feel calmer and less stressed. But you may be asking yourself how meditation can improve self-esteem and decrease neurotic and other self-destructive behaviors.

Meditation may just be the most effective psychotherapy available. Traditional psychotherapy focuses on dysfunctional behaviors and addresses immediate and intermediate causes. For example, if the dysfunctional behavior presented to the therapist is compulsive overeating, the therapy will probably examine those current situations that trigger the dysfunctional behavior and look at the client's childhood to discover factors, such as feeling unloved or equating food with love, to assist the client in understanding and changing the behavior. These factors are certainly part of the whole picture, but they are not the ultimate cause of the problem. The ultimate cause is in consciousness, and this is where meditation works — in the realm of awareness or consciousness.

Looking at an example in nature is helpful in understanding this concept. If you have a fruit tree that is not bearing fruit, you water and fertilize it. As the tree receives the nutrients it requires, all parts are healed — roots, trunk, sap, branches, leaves — as it is restored to its natural, productive nature. And in the appropriate season it blossoms and then bears its fruit.

Similarly, meditation nurtures at the core level, returning the self to its natural state of balance and harmony. Why do people overindulge in drugs, alcohol, sex, or food, or engage in other self-destructive behaviors? They are merely trying to feel good and are searching for that place of equilibrium, of wholeness, of peace.

Meditation is actually a reclaiming of those lost parts of self and an integration into a way of being that is not dependent on externals for happiness. As this new balance is achieved through going within, the behaviors that had appeared to be allies in achieving psychological well-being become revealed for what they really are — destructive of the true nature of the self.

As the meditative state and the feelings of peace and wholeness it brings become more integrated into the self, the need to search for external tranquilizers of one sort or another diminishes and, over time, usually ceases entirely. Meditators typically report that their addictive habits and self-destructive behaviors simply fall away without the exertion of any effort or willpower.

Psychologist Dr. Nathaniel Branden (1994), a prolific author in the area of self-esteem for three decades, addresses the importance of changing consciousness in his latest book, *The Six Pillars of Self-Esteem*. Becoming more aware or conscious, according to Branden, is the very first pillar for building self-esteem. With this cornerstone established, the other pillars can then be erected — self-acceptance, self-responsibility, self-assertiveness, purposeful living, and personal integrity. True change is an inside-out job and always begins with changing consciousness.

In the deeply relaxed state of alert awareness, the mind settles into a nonverbal state of being, where it accesses the backlog of subconscious unfinished business. As this psychic debris — the old hurts, misunderstandings, misconceptions — come to the surface and are released, perceptual reality changes. And this change in consciousness subsequently changes self-concept. With a healthier self-concept, positive transformation in external circumstances naturally occurs, just as a well-nourished tree naturally blossoms and bears its fruit.

MEDITATION, PRODUCTIVITY, AND CREATIVITY

Increased Productivity

One of the common reported effects of meditation is increased productivity. Meditators not only perform better than nonmeditators, as noted in the research described previously, but they typically are able to do more with less effort.

The comprehensive, integrated state of hypometabolic awareness is the complete opposite of a maladaptive, anxiety state. The experience is that of a refreshing state of restful alertness. The energy once tied up with worrying about the past, fearing the future, and being stressed in the present is now available for other uses. As the body adapts with continued practice to being in this calm but refreshed state, a new aliveness becomes possible. With more energy both available and accessible, tasks that once seemed cumbersome and tiresome now are performed quickly and effortlessly.

Enhanced Creativity

Those who meditate regularly notice that not only do they become more productive, but they become more creative as well. To understand this phenomenon, it is useful to look at both the type of brain waves exhibited during varying states of consciousness and at the functional qualities of different areas of the brain.

There are four categories of brain waves that operate at different frequencies. Beta waves, correlated with the active use of the five senses in such states as thinking, concentration, and tension, are the fastest at 14 to 22 cycles per second (cps). Alpha waves, discovered in the 1920s, are slower and larger with frequency waves of 7 to 14 cps and typically are observed when the eyes are closed and not processing externally generated visual information. Theta waves are slower than alpha, with a frequency of 4 to 7 cps. Delta waves are the slowest at 3 to 5 cps. Theta and delta waves are seen in adults during drowsiness and quiet sleep, and theta waves are evident during states of creativity and serene pleasure.

When you move into a meditative state, the brain slows from active beta mentation to the slower alpha waves and sometimes even to the still slower theta waves. Alpha waves are associated more with the right hemisphere of the brain, the section of the brain that thinks holistically and intuitively. In moving from the beta to the alpha frequency, attention is shifted from the logical, analytical left hemisphere to the nonlinear, nonverbal, artistic right hemisphere.

Another interesting brain wave phenomenon has been observed in meditators. During meditation alpha waves spread synchronously from the back to the front of the brain and between the right and left hemispheres. This hypersynchronicity is unique to the meditative state, as brain waves are random and chaotic during ordinary waking consciousness.

This integration of the two hemispheres and the limbic and cortical areas of the brain brings together the emotions and reason, the analytical and the intuitive, into a wholeness capable of enhanced creativity. In this state of "combinatory play," so aptly named by Albert Einstein, undreamed of possibilities are revealed. This is the realm of genius, pure inspiration, and invention. And this realm is available to everyone, not just a select few.

References

Abrams, A. I. (1974). Paired associate learning and recall. In D. W. Orme-Johnson, L. H. Domash, & J. T. Farrow (Eds.), *Scientific research on transcendental meditation: Collected papers.* Los Angeles: MIU Press.

Benson, H. (1969). Yoga for drug abuse. *New England Journal of Medicine, 281*(20), 1133.

Benson, H., & Wallace, R. K. (1972). Decreased drug abuse with transcendental meditation: A study of 1,862 subjects. In D. J. D. Azrafonetis (Ed.), *Proceedings of the international symposium on drug abuse* (pp. 369–376). Philadelphia: Lea and Febiger.

Blasdell, K. (1974). The effect of transcendental meditation upon a complex perceptual motor test. In D. W. Orme-Johnson, L. H. Domash, & J. T. Farrow (Eds.), *Scientific research on transcendental meditation: Collected papers.* Los Angeles: MIU Press.

Boese, E., & Berger, K. (1972). In search of a fourth state of consciousness: Psychological and physiological correlates of meditation. (Research paper). Pennsylvania State University Medical School.

Branden, Nathaniel. (1994). *The six pillars of self-esteem.* New York: Bantam.

Brown, F. M., Stewart, W. S., & Blodgett, J. T. (1971, November 13). *EEG kappa rhythms during transcendental meditation and possible perceptual threshold changes following.* Presented to the Kentucky Academy of Sciences, Richmond, KY. Revised January 1972.

Fehr, T., Nerstherimer, U., & Torber, S. (1974). Study of 49 practitioners of transcendental meditation with Freiburger Personality Inventory. In D. W. Orme-Johnson, L. H. Domash, & J. T. Farrow (Eds.), *Scientific research on transcedental meditation: Collected papers.* Los Angeles: MIU Press.

Gelderloss, P., Hermans, H. J., Ahlserom, H. H., & Jacoby, R. (1990, March). Transcendence and psychological health: Studies with long-term participants of the transcendental meditation and TM-Sidhi programs. *Journal of Psychology, 124*(2), 177–197.

Graham, J. (1974). Auditory discrimination in meditators. In D. W. Orme-Johnson, L. H. Domash, & J. T. Farrow (Eds.), *Scientific research on transcendental meditation: Collected papers.* Los Angeles: MIU Press.

Hjelle, L. A. (1972). *Transcendental meditation and psychological health.* (Research paper). Department of Psychology, State University College, Brockport, NY.

Kabat-Zinn, J., Massion, A. O., Kristeller, J., Peterson, L. G., & Fletcher, K. E. (1992, July). Effectiveness of a meditation-based stress reduction program in the treatment of anxiety disorders. *American Journal of Psychiatry, 149*(7), 936–943.

Nidich, S., Seeman, W., & Dreskin, T. (1974). Influence of transcendental meditation: A replication. *Journal of Counseling Psychology.*

Orme-Johnson, D. W. (1974). Transcendental meditation for drug abuse counselors. In D. W. Orme-Johnson, L. H. Domash, & J. T. Farrow (Eds.), *Scientific research on transcendental meditation: Collected papers.* Los Angeles: MIU Press.

Pelletier, K. R. (1972). Altered attention deployment in meditators. (Research paper). Psychology Clinic, University of California, Berkeley.

Shapiro, D. H. (1992). A mode of control and self-control profile for long-term meditators. *Psychologia: An International Journal of Psychology in the Orient, 35*(n1), 1–11.

Shelly, M. W. (summarized by G. Landrith). (1972). A theory of happiness as it relates to transcendental meditation. (Research paper). Department of Psychology, University of Kansas, Lawrence, KS.

Tsai, S. L., & Crockett, M. S. (1993, January–March). Effects of relaxation training, combining imagery and meditation on the stress level of Chinese nurses in modern hospitals in Taiwan. *Issues in Mental Health Nursing, 14*(1), 51–66.

Winquist, W. T. (1969). The effects of the regular practice of transcendental meditation on students involved in the regular use of hallucinogenic and "hard" drugs. (Research paper). Department of Sociology, University of California at Los Angeles.

4 TYPES OF MEDITATIVE PRACTICE

Many paths lead to the same destination.

A VARIETY FROM WHICH TO CHOOSE

There are many different types of meditative practice. Although the techniques may vary, no one way is any better than another. As each person is unique, the choice of meditative technique is a personal one. What is comfortable for one person may be completely unsuitable for another. Also, what is compatible with you at one point on your spiritual journey may not suit you at another point.

Regardless of how different the techniques may appear, the purpose of each one is the same — to connect you to that which is larger than the individual self. Meditation provides you with an approach to entering the silence, the place at the center of life that is motionless. This is the place of pure awareness, creativity, and regeneration.

This chapter presents an introduction to a variety of meditative practices; chapter 6 provides step-by-step instructions on four of the techniques.

CONCENTRATION

Meditation is a state of concentrated or focused attention. The mind is deeply relaxed but alert and one-pointed in its focus. The mind is fixed on a specific task or object. When it wanders, it is gently brought back to center. A number of techniques have been used traditionally to develop and deepen concentration.

Candle Flame

In this experience you simply focus your attention on the flame of a candle. As thoughts arise that distract you from the focus, you notice them and let them pass from your awareness, gently coaxing your attention back to the candle flame.

Breath

This is a concentration technique that centers the attention on the movement of the breath in and out of the body, while you sit relaxed in a meditative posture with eyes closed. Variations of this exercise include simply noticing the movement of the breath, counting breaths, or subvocalizing one word on the inhale and another on the exhale.

Mantra

Mantra is Sanskrit for a word or phrase that is subvocalized or vocalized repeatedly as a mechanism for centering attention. It is one of the most widely used forms of meditation and is found in almost every major mystical tradition. Some common Christian mantras include the Hail, Mary, "Christ have mercy," and the Latin *"Deus in adjutorium meum intende"* ("Oh, God, come to my aid"). Common mantras from the East include the Sanskrit *"aum,"* the one basic sound that is the totality of all sound, and *"jai Ram,"* praising God. The Sufi *"Allah hu"* honors Islam's supreme being, Allah.

In mantra meditation the centering device is the internal repetition of a word or short phrase, either secular or one with spiritual significance. Teachings based on mystical traditions, however, instruct that only a spiritually significant or sacred mantra be used for this meditation. It is believed that there is spiritual power in both the content and the vibrational tone of such words. Chapter 6 looks at some American research that also supports the selection of a spiritually imbued mantra.

CONTEMPLATION

Contemplation is yet another form of meditation. To contemplate is to observe with continued attention. Contemplation is an allowing of the mind to become one with an idea or an image in a centered but floating way, sort of a focused reverie. Communing with nature and deeply considering spiritual writings are common forms of practice.

A Tibetan Buddhist technique involves the focusing of attention on complex tapestries of deities who represent various qualities of God. Aspirants can spend as long as 3 or 4 years contemplating just one of these deities. The Zen Buddhists use koans, a type of riddle, for contemplation. One of the best-known koans in the Western world is, "What is the sound of one hand clapping?"

DEVOTION

Devotional practices are another common form of meditation. Devotion is the path of the heart, a feeling of love for God, a deity, saint, or other representative of divine qualities. Devotion is the path through the emotions and is practiced by all traditions, including Christian monastics in the Western world and students of *Bhakti-Yoga* in the East.

The focus of devotion may be a living being such as a guru, saint, or other perceived enlightened being. In the Hindu tradition group gatherings called *satsang* are held with such teachers. A common practice during these gatherings is *kirtan* — the singing of devotional chants.

Devotional worship also occurs with images or statues of divine figures such as Christ, Virgin Mary, Krishna, Buddha, and so forth, or in churches or temples where these beings are exalted.

MINDFULNESS

Mindfulness is the process of giving full attention to everything you do. It is being like a child who is totally present in the moment with everything she is experiencing. It is a way of moving in the world in an eyes-open meditative state of awareness.

MOVEMENT

For those who have trouble sitting still or for those who want to add variety to their meditative practices, a variety of moving techniques are available. These techniques reach that still center of being through a combination of controlled breathing or mantra chanting and movement.

Hatha Yoga

Yoga, a Sanskrit word meaning "bringing together as one" or "union," is an ancient Hindu approach to living a balanced life. *Hatha yoga* is a practice of the yoga tradition that combines gentle stretching postures *(asanas)* with controlled breathing *(pranayama)*. Translated from the Hindi, *hatha yoga* means "sun and moon" and is a moving meditative practice for achieving balance between the male, active energies (sun) and the female, receptive energies (moon). During the practice of the postures the mind is focused on the breath as the body stretches, releasing tensions and coming to a more balanced state.

T'ai Chi

T'ai chi is an oriental martial art that is in itself a meditative practice of movement. Through a series of controlled graceful movements and calmness of breath, practitioners move their energy *(chi)*. What appears to be a slow-motion dance requires intense concentration and meditative focus.

Sufi Dancing

Perhaps the best known of the Sufi dances is the whirling of the dervishes who spin themselves into a state of altered consciousness. There are, however, a variety of other dances and walks practiced by the Sufis. The movement is typically combined with inspirational chanting, bringing participants into a deepening meditative state as the dancing proceeds.

SELECTING YOUR PATH

The path you should choose is only known to you. Go with what appeals to you. If no one method calls you, practice a variety, allowing yourself 2 to 3 weeks to fully experience each one. Also, allow yourself the freedom to change. A method that may be a good beginning one for you may not feel as sustaining later on, or you may want to combine a sitting technique with a moving one.

Suggested Reading

Kahn, S., & Saulo, M. (1994). *Healing yourself: A nurse's guide to self-care and renewal.* Albany, NY: Delmar Publishers Inc.

Le Shan, L. (1979). *How to meditate: A guide to self discovery* (9th ed.). Boston: Little, Brown.

Ram Daas. (1990). *Journey of awakening: A meditator's guidebook.* New York: Bantam.

5 | PREPARING FOR MEDITATION

A strong foundation provides a stable base upon which to build your new house.

CORNERSTONES OF MEDITATION

This chapter will provide you with pragmatic exercises to give you a preview of the two, distinct components of meditation, relaxation and concentration, that are the cornerstones of the practice. Although general guidelines for meditation are provided here, specific instructions for different types of meditative practices are included in chapter 6.

Two distinct activities are involved in meditation regardless of the method: concentration and relaxation. Concentration is simply a focusing of attention or energy upon a selected object. It is not effortful; it gently consolidates or centers attention so that all energy is directed to a single point of awareness. Relaxation is a state of calmness where there is an absence of tension: physical, emotional, and mental. Meditation is a combined experience of deep relaxation and alert, focused attention.

RELAXATION

Most people move through their days with some level of tension. Even when you think you are relaxed, you really are not. You are usually just a little less tense than you were before you "relaxed." Because the

experience of true relaxation is foreign to many, an exercise to assist
you in kinesthetically experiencing relaxation follows. Exercise 5.1
gives you a preview of the deep relaxation you can experience in
meditation. If someone is interested in assisting you, ask that person
to read the instructions to you. If you are alone, you might want to
make an audiotape to play back to yourself, or you may simply read
the instructions a couple of times before you begin.

EXERCISE 5.1

Body Relaxation[1]

1. Before you begin the exercise, take a 10-second pulse, record it, and set the paper aside until the end of the exercise.

2. Lie comfortably on the floor on your back with your eyes closed.

3. Take a few deep breaths, breathing from the diaphragm rather than from the chest.

4. Tense your right arm and hand, make a fist with your hand, and hold for a count of 15.

5. Totally relax your right arm and hand. Breathe slowly and deeply for a count of 15.

6. Tense your right buttock, leg, and foot, and hold for a count of 15.

7. Completely release your right buttock, leg, and foot. Breathe slowly and deeply for a count of 15.

8. Tense your left arm and hand, make a fist with your hand, and hold for a count of 15.

9. Totally relax your left arm and hand. Breathe slowly and deeply for a count of 15.

10. Tense your left buttock, leg, and foot, and hold for a count of 15.

11. Completely release your left buttock, leg, and foot. Breathe slowly and deeply for a count of 15.

12. Tense your entire body, including your face, for a count of 15.

13. Release your entire body, making an "aah" sound as you do so.

[1] From *Healing Yourself: A Nurse's Guide to Self-Care and Renewal* by S. Kahn and M. Saulo, 1994, Albany, NY: Delmar Publishers Inc. Adapted by permission.

14. Lie quietly and breathe slowly. Scan your body, moving your awareness from your toes, through your torso, and all the way up to the top of your head. Experience what it feels like to be completely relaxed.

15. Before you get up, take another 10-second pulse. When you compare it to the pulse you took before you began this exercise, you will probably find that it is slower now that you are relaxed.

CONCENTRATION

All too often people associate concentration with intensity or effort. "Don't bother me, I have to really concentrate on this problem" or "I'm concentrating as hard as I can" are statements reflecting this common belief. But concentration is simply focusing of attention. The act of concentrating is directive rather than forceful. All forms of meditation involve concentration; attention is focused on breathing, mantra repetition, movement, chanting, and so forth.

Exercise 5.2 uses a rose as a point of focus. As you are engaging in this process, it is important to be aware of the activity of your mind. It is very common for the mind to wander from its point of concentration. If you find your mind drifting into thoughts other than those that relate to the specific activity of observing the rose, gently bring it back to the task at hand. Do not force it back; rather, guide it as you would a small child who has wandered off the trail during a group hike.

As in the relaxation exercise, you may choose to have someone assist you, record the instructions on audiotape, or read them to yourself a couple of times before you begin. Particularly if you have someone reading the instructions or you record them on tape, be sure to allow adequate time for each step in the process.

EXERCISE 5.2

Rose Concentration[2]

1. Obtain a rose that is partially open.

2. Allowing the rose to rest in one of your hands, sit comfortably in a quiet space and close your eyes for a minute.

---

[2] From *Healing Yourself: A Nurse's Guide to Self-Care and Renewal* by S. Kahn and M. Saulo, 1994, Albany, NY: Delmar Publishers Inc. Adapted by permission.

3. Open your eyes and look at the rose and nothing else.

4. Focus your attention first on one petal. Notice the color, texture, size, and shape of the petal.

5. Now, move your attention from that petal to the adjacent one. Examine this petal with the same focused interest. Continue this process for each petal, noting how each one is the same and yet different from the previous one.

6. After you have examined all of the petals, notice every small detail of each leaf on the stem, then move on to the stem itself, and finally study any thorns present on the stem.

7. Now, move the rose a short distance away from you and look at the flower in its completeness. Note its overall shape, form, color, and texture.

8. Smell the fragrance, taking a few slow, deep breaths. Then close your eyes and concentrate solely on the fragrance.

9. Open your eyes, take in the complete rose one more time, and inhale its fragrance.

10. Now, close your eyes, rest the rose once again in one hand, and take the image of the rose into your heart. With your eyes closed, continue to smell the rose and see it in as much detail as you can with your mind's eye.

11. Slowly open your eyes, take a few deep breaths, and notice how you feel.

GENERAL GUIDELINES FOR MEDITATION

If you have pictures in your mind of a meditator wearing long, flowing white robes and sitting in a complex, double-jointed position on a tree-covered mountaintop, just let them pass right on through. Meditation does not require any special equipment, and it can be practiced anywhere and anytime. However, as is true with the adoption of any new habit or the acquiring of any new skill, there are some practical guidelines that can be of assistance to you as you begin your practice.

Creating Your Sacred Space

It is very helpful in developing the meditative habit to create a place in your residence that becomes your designated meditative space. This can be as expansive as a room or a portion of a room that you use only for meditation or as simple as selecting a chair, a section of a couch, or a corner of a room with a cushion on the floor.

Arrange your space so it is clean, orderly, and comfortable. If there is a telephone or answering machine in your meditation area, make sure the sound is turned off so that you will not be distracted should it ring while you are meditating.

You may want to place sacred objects in your space such as gemstones, flowers, or pictures of spiritual leaders, saints, or other individuals who inspire you. Burning candles and incense are other common practices people employ to create a spiritualized atmosphere for themselves.

Also, see if you can find a space on your unit that can be used for meditation. An empty patient room or an infrequently used storage room may be able to serve that purpose. Or perhaps there is a corner in a courtyard or other outside area where you can sit in silence. And if you have the good fortune of being involved in the design or redesign of a unit, plan for a quiet room that can be used by staff, patients, and their friends and families.

Establishing a Routine

It is also important to set aside a specified time for meditation. Again, this is a way to provide structure and discipline while you are developing a new habit.

Before breakfast and before bedtime are common meditation times in many spiritual traditions. These times are valued for setting the tone for the beginning and the ending of each day with periods of spiritual communion. Another reason for selecting these times is that typically the body is not busy digesting food, which distracts some energy from the meditation.

Whatever time periods you do select for meditation, it is best not to eat 2 hours prior to your practice so that you can concentrate your complete energy on your meditation. However, do not forgo meditation because you have recently eaten. And if you are very hungry when you sit down to meditate and your stomach is growling and gurgling, take a glass of juice or a piece of fruit. Being physically uncomfortable can be as distracting as being too full.

As the old Chinese saying goes, "The longest journey begins with the first step." Because most people have restless minds that are not used to being quiet and focused, it is best to start with a meditation of 5 minutes unless you are initially able to be still for a longer period. Gradually condition your mind just as you condition your body when you begin a physical training program. When you are comfortable with that 5 minutes, add small time bites until you build up to 20- to 30-minute periods once or twice a day.

Body Positioning

In any sitting meditative practice, it is important that the spine be erect but relaxed. One way to achieve this is to find a chair or firm couch that is comfortable and suits your body, so that your back is straight and your feet rest comfortably on the floor. Or you may choose to sit in a cross-legged position on the floor. Some place pillows under their "sit-bones" to create stable bases for themselves. There are also wooden meditation benches available that create the same effect. What is most important is to find a way of positioning your body that is specifically comfortable for you.

Another important aspect of being comfortable in your body is to wear clothing that is nonrestrictive, particularly around the abdominal area. This can be as simple as undoing your belt or unbuttoning your waistband to allow sufficient space.

Once you have found a comfortable position for yourself and released any restrictive apparel, your hands should be placed palms-up in an open, receptive position, resting the back of your hands upon your thighs. Your body is now positioned for meditation. Chapter 6 will provide you with instructions in a variety of techniques you may use for a sitting meditation.

6 MEDITATIVE TECHNIQUES

It is how you do what you do rather than what you do that makes a difference.

THE HOW OF WHAT YOU DO

As was described in chapter 4, a variety of meditative techniques are available. Some are structured, some unstructured; some are utilized with eyes open, others with eyes closed. Many are sitting practices, some involve chanting and dancing, and still others focus attention with stretching and breathing.

In meditation it matters not so much what you do but rather how you do it. The how for any chosen practice combines consistency and persistence with compassion. As with the acquiring of any new habit or skill, consistency is most important in building spiritual "muscles." Daily practice, even if just for 5 minutes, begins to cut a new groove in your consciousness. The self-discipline to continue despite seeming distractions and obstacles is also very important. Commitment to your practice and your spiritual growth will serve you well; this will become evident over time as you experience the fruits of your dedication.

However, at the same time, it is important to be compassionate with yourself. Too frequently, you can be your own worst critic. You will occasionally slip and slide a bit, and consistency and persistence may appear to be only abstract concepts. This is the time to be compassionate and forgiving with yourself. Look at your humanness, your resistances, and your fears. Bless them, release them, and move on once more.

A VARIETY OF TECHNIQUES

Although there are many ways to meditate, this chapter will limit itself to providing instruction on a few techniques that can be easily self-taught. Three of the four techniques described — breath meditation, mantra meditation, and contemplation — are sitting practices. The fourth technique, mindfulness, is a meditative activity that can be engaged in either sitting or moving, depending on what is the focus of attention.

All techniques are designed to enable you to develop dominion over your attention. Although it is important to practice the techniques in accordance with the instructions provided, your intention behind the practice is even more important than the technique itself. Any technique should be engaged in with the intention of unity of your small self with your higher self, God, the universe, the unified field — whatever it is you choose to call it. The power of your intention, your desire for the merging, will carry you through any imperfections in your technique.

Thought Watching

One common experience that beginning meditators experience regardless of the method selected is the busyness of their minds. You sit down to meditate, but rather than focusing on your chosen object of attention, your mind is very busy thinking. You may be thinking about what you are going to do after you finish meditating, remembering what happened yesterday, planning your next meal, or worrying about your finances.

It is important to realize that thoughts are not your awareness. An ancient Buddhist sage drew an analogy between thoughts moving in the mind and clouds moving in the sky. He noted that clouds move easily from one place to another. They are not attached to anything; they simply are in one place and then in another. They do not grow roots and become attached to a stationary position in the sky. Similarly, it is important to not hold onto thoughts. Just let them pass on through your mind, and gently bring your awareness back to your chosen focus of attention — the breath, a mantra, and so forth.

BREATH

The Power of the Breath

In the Western world, very little attention is paid to breathing. It is viewed as simply an automatic process that maintains the oxygenation of the body. The importance of breathing may temporarily come to your awareness during occasions of physical exertion or when you are experiencing extreme stress, but generally breathing and its continual function are taken for granted.

The Eastern traditions, however, have given far more importance to the breath than its physiological function. The Chinese associate breathing with the flow of *chi,* or energy, through the system of *meridians* (energy passageways) in the body. The moving meditation of t'ai chi and other forms of Chinese exercise and martial arts consciously use the breath as an integral component of the practices.

In India, breathing is associated with *prana,* the life force of the body and the source of all vitality and well-being. Yoga, the comprehensive Indian approach to living a balanced life, specifically designates *pranayama* — the understanding and control of the breath — as one of its eight disciplines. The appropriate use of the breath is also an integral component of the practice of hatha yoga.

Diaphragmatic Breathing

The typical breathing pattern of a stressful lifestyle is shallow, chest breathing, which does not provide complete aeration of the lungs nor adequate oxygenation of the blood. The far more efficient way to breathe is from the diaphragm, which brings in 8 times as much air as does chest breathing.

This slower, deeper diaphragmatic or abdominal breathing pattern balances the sympathetic and parasympathetic nervous systems, bringing the body into a state of peace and calmness, while at the same time improving cellular oxygenation, metabolism, and elimination. In the animal kingdom, the tortoise, which breathes just 3 times per minute, far outlives the excitable monkey and the active hen, which breathe about 30 times per minute.

Because diaphragmatic breathing is the correct mode for the practice of breath meditation, it may be useful for you to experience this pattern before entering into the meditation by following the instructions in exercise 6.1.

EXERCISE 6.1

Diaphragmatic Breathing

1. Sit comfortably with your back erect but relaxed.

2. Rest your right hand on your abdomen, your left hand on your chest, and close your eyes.

3. Inhale deeply through your nose and exhale through your nose, allowing your abdominal muscles to contract on the exhale.

4. Your right hand should rise upon inhale and fall with the exhale.

5. Allow your breath to flow easily finding a rhythm that is comfortable for you, and make sure that you do not retain the breath between the inhale and the exhale.

Breath Meditation

Now that you are familiar with abdominal breathing, you are ready to experience breath meditation. Follow the instructions in exercise 6.2. Allow 5 minutes for this first experience. You may want to set a timer in another room so that you will not be distracted by the ticking sounds, or you may simply look at a clock or watch when you begin and when you end. Once you have clocked yourself a few times, you will find that your body will begin to have a memory of what 5 minutes feels like. Gradually work up to 20 to 30 minutes once or twice a day.

EXERCISE 6.2[1]

Breath Meditation

1. Sit comfortably in a meditative position and close your eyes.

2. Breathe abdominally, allowing your breath to move effortlessly in and out through your nose, making sure you are not holding your breath between the inhalation and exhalation.

---

[1] From *Healing Yourself: A Nurse's Guide to Self-Care and Renewal* by S. Kahn and M. Saulo, 1994, Albany, NY: Delmar Publishers Inc. Adapted by permission.

3. Repeat this a few moments until you become comfortable with your own rhythm.

4. Now, move your full attention to the flow of your breath, thinking "in" as you inhale and "out" as you exhale.

5. Continue focusing on the movement of your breath. If your mind should be distracted by thoughts, gently bring it back to the in and out of your breath.

MANTRA

As discussed in chapter 4, mantra is a Sanskrit term meaning the repetition of a sacred word or phrase as a form of devotional invocation. It is a common form of meditation in both the Eastern and Western traditions.

In a broader sense, mantra may be defined as affirmative thought. An affirmation is a declaration of a positive truth, and its repetition reprograms your consciousness to align with the declaration. Attention follows thought. You can begin to see, then, how the repetition of a mantra merges your consciousness with the content and intent of the phrase or word.

Mantra meditation may be done with either a spiritually significant or secular word or phrase. As discussed in chapter 4, mystical traditions use sacred words because of both their content and their vibrational tone. Contemporary American research by Dr. Herbert Benson on mantra meditators (1984) supports this practice. He found that the use of a faith-related mantra was ultimately more effective than a secular one. When Benson requested his patients to select a mantra, 80% chose a spiritual phrase or word, and the remaining 20% made a secular choice. Those using a spiritual mantra showed greater health improvement and longer participation in the program than did those who used a secular mantra.

Preparing for Mantra Meditation

To prepare for mantra meditation, select a phrase or word that brings a peaceful feeling to you. One of the most common spiritual mantras used is *aum* (pronounced "om"), which is a Sanskrit word meaning one. In addition to the concept of unity expressed in the content of the word, many in the spiritual world feel that the sound of the word has a vibrational quality that also expresses its concept — the *a* is the sound of the heart and the *um* the sound of the mind. The unique tonal quality of this word creates a unity between the heart and mind. For several reasons, then, *aum* is a particularly powerful mantra for meditation.

Depending on your religious background or spiritual affiliation, you might feel drawn to God, Allah, Jesus Christ, shalom, aloha, or amen as a mantra. If you are more oriented to the secular world, words such as ocean, relax, wisdom, or peace may appeal to you.

Phrases, particularly those that begin with "I am," are potent mantras. "I am love," "I am light," or "I am the same essence as is God," are a few examples. "*Sri Ram, jai Ram, jai jai Ram*" is a Sanskrit mantra that loosely translates to "Sacred God, glory to God, glory, glory to God." The biblical phrase, "I am the way, the truth, and the light" is yet another wonderful mantra.

Mantra Meditation

The general instructions in exercise 6.3 are similar to those for breath meditation. Start with 5 minutes and work up to longer sessions. Stay with the same mantra for 2 to 3 weeks, but change it after that as you feel moved to do so.

EXERCISE 6.3 [2]

Mantra Meditation

1. Bring to mind the mantra you will be focusing upon in your meditation.

2. Sit comfortably in a meditative position and close your eyes.

3. Initially, focus your attention on your breath, breathing abdominally in a slow and steady pattern that is comfortable for you.

4. Now, move your attention to your mantra while you continue to breathe slowly and effortlessly.

---

[2] From *Healing Yourself: A Nurse's Guide to Self-Care and Renewal* by S. Kahn and M. Saulo, 1994, Albany, NY: Delmar Publishers Inc. Adapted by permission.

5. Upon each exhale of your breath, speak your selected word or phrase either aloud or silently.

6. Continue repeating your mantra, gently bringing your attention back to it should your mind wander.

CONTEMPLATION

As discussed in chapter 4, contemplation is a sort of inspired reverie. In this type of meditation, attention is focused upon nature, an object, or an inspirational writing. Henry Thoreau, author of *Walden* (1989), described his nature contemplation thusly:

> Sometimes, I sat in my sunny doorway from sunrise till noon, rapt in a revery, amidst the pines and hickories and sumacs, in undisturbed solitude and stillness, while the birds sang around or flitted noiseless through the house, until by the sun falling in at my west window, or the noise of a traveller's wagon on the distant highway, I was reminded of the pass of time.

Or you may choose to contemplate upon a passage from the Bible, the Bhagavad Gita, or any other spiritually inspired writing, such as the following excerpt from Christian D. Larson's *Pathway of the Roses* (1993):

> Live a beautiful life wherever you may be and you become a living benediction to all who may pass your way. You may see no immediate results; in fact, your beautiful life may have scattered its blessings so far and wide that you cannot find the exact places where the flowers grow that you have planted; but that does not matter. You have given; in consequence, the world is better off and you are a stronger soul.

Contemplative Nature Meditation

In contemplating nature, enter into a quiet space with slow, abdominal breathing, allowing your eyes to relax into a soft focus. Then simply observe what is around you from this place of relaxed but focused attention. For example, let your eyes rest on the trees and allow your ears to tune to the sounds of nature around you — the birds singing, the movement of the leaves in the breeze, the concert of the frogs and crickets, or the lazy fall of the water as it allows gravity to pull it from the top of the mountain into the stream. Watch with the same intensity of interest the play of the sun as it creates shadows on the ground and the changing of those shadows as the sun moves ever so slightly in its orbit.

Allow yourself to merge with the object of your observation — see it, feel it, sense it, know it. If you should feel your mind drift off your focus or if distracting thoughts pull you away, just observe what is happening in your mind, and bring your awareness back once more to the object of your contemplation.

Contemplative Reading Meditation

In entering into a contemplative meditation of a spiritually inspired written passage, simply close your eyes after having read it a time or two. Do not try to memorize the words but rather catch the essence of the meaning, and let your meditation focus on that essence. Feel the energy and intention of the passage rather than thinking about the specific words, and let your consciousness become one with them. As with the nature contemplation, if you become distracted from the object of your contemplation, gently move your awareness back to the essence of the passage.

The last part of this book contains weekly sets of journal pages, each of which includes a brief inspirational statement. Contemplating the statements is one way in which that section may be used. This process is described in more detail in chapter 11.

MINDFULNESS

Mindfulness is a Buddhist practice of focusing your attention on one activity and remaining focused fully on that activity. You have a penetrating awareness of each moment. The Japanese Zen practices of flower arranging, archery, and tea ceremonies are examples of open-eye mindfulness meditations. Walking and eating are other examples of activities that are used for open-eye mindfulness meditation, and observing thoughts is a mindfulness meditation that is done with closed eyes. Instructions follow for both a thought-watching and eating meditation.

Thought-Watching Mindfulness Meditation

This meditative technique varies somewhat from earlier techniques in its approach to the appearance of thoughts in your meditation. In the other techniques, you were instructed to not focus on the thoughts as they appeared, but rather to just let them pass from your consciousness and return to your breathing, mantra, and so on. In the mindfulness technique described in exercise 6.4 you place your awareness on the thought without analyzing or judging it, and you simply watch as it disappears from your mind.

EXERCISE 6.4

Thought-Watching Mindfulness Meditation

1. Sit comfortably in a meditative position with closed eyes and breathe abdominally.

2. Focus on your breathing, noting to yourself "in" and "out" with the movement of your breath.

3. When thoughts distract you from focusing on your breathing, mentally note the thought and say "thinking" to yourself.

4. Observe your thought without getting involved in the content or analyzing or judging it. Watch it dissolve as you focus your attention on "thinking."

5. Continue your meditation focusing on the breath and repeat the process of mentally noting "thinking" each time a thought arises. Watch it pass away, and return continually to watching your breath.

Eating Mindfulness Meditation

The focus of attention in exercise 6.5 is on all the subtle activities involved in eating. If your awareness should wander, gently guide it back and refocus on eating.

EXERCISE 6.5

Eating Mindfulness Meditation

1. Take a plate with a variety of foods and place it before you on a table.

2. Sit in your chair and close your eyes for a moment, taking a few deep, slow breaths.

3. Open your eyes and look at the food, noticing the colors, the textures, the arrangement on the plate and so on.

4. Inhale deeply, taking in the aromas of the food. Focus your attention on each individual food and note the differences among them.

5. Pick up your fork slowly, being conscious of how your hand is lifting the fork and mentally note "lifting."

6. Gather up a forkful of food and as you do so mentally note "gathering."

7. Lift the forkful of food slowly to your mouth and note, once again, "lifting."

8. Open your mouth slowly and place the food in your mouth, mentally noting "placing."

9. Close your mouth and lower your fork, noting "lowering." Place it on your plate and notice its position.

10. Begin to chew the food slowly noticing the texture, the flavor, the feel of the food on your tongue and on your teeth as it is being chewed. Notice every detail of the activity.

11. When the food has been chewed sufficiently, swallow what is in your mouth paying full attention to how it feels as it moves down your throat.

12. Continue eating the rest of your meal in this manner being mindful of every activity.

References

Benson, H., & Proctor, W. (1984). *Beyond the relaxation response*. New York: Time Books.

Larson, C. (1993). *The pathway of roses.* Lakewood, CA: Mannahouse Publishing.

Thoreau, H. (1989). *Walden.* Princeton: Princeton University Press.

Suggested Reading

Harp, D. (1990). *The new three minute meditation.* Oakland, CA: New Harbinger Publications.

Kabat-Zinn, J. (1994). *Wherever you go there you are: Mindfulness meditation in everyday life.* New York: Hyperion.

Kornfield, J., & Goldstein, J. (1987). *Seeking the heart of wisdom.* Boston: Shambhala Publications.

Le Shan, L. (1979). *How to meditate: A guide to self discovery* (9th ed.). Boston: Little, Brown.

Ram Daas. (1990). *Journey of awakening: A meditator's guidebook.* New York: Bantam.

Swami Rama. (1992). *Meditation and its practice.* Homesdale, PA: Himalayan International Institute.

7 | MOVING DEEPER

The universe is limitless.

INTERNAL TOOLS

Once you have developed a habit of meditating 20 or 30 minutes a day, you may want to move deeper in your practice. This chapter will provide you with some ways to do so.

Deep Breathing

In earlier chapters you were provided instruction in how to breathe diaphragmatically or abdominally. An extension of this type of breathing is a form of *pranayama* yoga practice involving slow, deep breathing. This breathing pattern has three components — inhalation, retention, and exhalation. Breathing this way prior to beginning your meditation can move you into a deeper space.

Yogis have developed a specific ratio for deep breathing of inhaling for 1 unit of time, retaining the breath for 4 units, and exhaling for 2 units (1:4:2). The extended retention of the breath allows for the diffusion of oxygen-rich air into the stale air residing in the lungs, and the deep exhalation removes more of the stale air than does a normal breathing pattern.

To give yourself an initial experience of this pattern, do not be concerned about the ratio. Place your body in a meditative position, close your eyes, and inhale deeply, feeling your abdomen fill with air.

Continue inhaling, feeling your chest expand and then your collarbone rise as you fill your lungs.

Retain your breath for as long as is comfortable, then begin to release it slowly in the reverse order of your inhale. Let the air first pass from your lungs, then observe it moving from your chest, and finally from your abdomen, contracting your abdominal muscles to complete the expulsion of air.

To work up to the 1:4:2 ratio, you may want to begin with a 1:1:1 inhale, retain, exhale ratio, employing the same technique you just experienced. Inhale for a count of 4, retain the breath for a count of 4, and then release it for a count of 4. You may then want to move to a 1:2:2 ratio, inhaling for a count of 4 and holding and exhaling the breath for a count of 8. For the 1:4:2 ratio the pattern is: inhale for a count of 4, hold your breath for a count of 16, and exhale for a count of 8.

Breathing deeply for 5 minutes prior to your meditation can move you easily into a stiller, deeper meditation. It is also useful when you are feeling restless, agitated, or stressed in your daily life.

Auming

You may recall from chapter 6 that the Sanskrit word *aum* has a vibrational quality that connects the heart with the mind. It is also a universal sound that encompasses all other sounds and thus establishes an atmosphere of unity. Because of these qualities the repetition of *aum* 21 times can move you to a level of deeper integration. You may choose to continue using the *aum* as your meditative focal point or you may move to watching your breath after you have completed the *aum* repetition.

Twirling

Remember spinning like a top when you were a child until everything started moving around you and you collapsed to the ground? This spinning or twirling is a meditative technique used by the Sufis. It seems to move you out of your left brain and free you of binding restrictions that may be placing limitations on the depth of your meditation.

Before you sit down to meditate, extend your arms parallel to the ground like a child who is pretending to be an airplane. Close your eyes and twirl in a clockwise direction 21 times. When you finish, immediately sit down and enter into your meditation.

Music

Just as continually chanting *aum* creates a vibrational quality conducive to meditation, certain types of music have a similar effect. Classical music by composers such as Pachelbel, Vivaldi, and Teleman can create an elevating atmosphere for your meditation. New Age music such as nature sounds, flute, harp, synthesized space journeys, and Gregorian chants are available on audio cassettes and CDs in most larger music stores. Other more esoteric music is available from metaphysical bookstores and catalogues. The music you select is a personal choice. Just make sure it is of a quality that deepens you rather than distracts you during the meditation.

Thought Specifying

In the preceding chapter you were instructed to watch your thoughts as they arose when you meditated, but not to judge them. Once you have established that watchfulness pattern, you may want to categorize, without judgment, the types of thoughts you are having as they pass through. This is a way of deepening your awareness of the nature of your thoughts.

One way you may want to categorize your thoughts is in terms of the time frame in which they exist. Simply notice in what time frame the thought exists as it passes through your awareness. For example, "That was a great movie last night," is a thought that exists in past time. "Will I have enough money to take care of my unexpected car repair?" is an example of a thought that exists in future time.

As each thought passes through, simply note to yourself "past" or "future" without judging or holding onto the thought. Simply observe what time category it falls into. One of the objectives of meditation is to train your mind to exist totally in the present moment. Seeing where the bulk of your thoughts are concentrated should assist you in becoming aware of where your energy is being other than in the present time. If you have thoughts that are in the present such as "I'm bored" or "I'm hungry," these are indications of a resistance to existing in the timeless, thoughtless state of meditation. Again, just watch them and let them move through without judgment.

Another way to become aware of thought patterns is to categorize them according to emotional quality. Again, do not judge or analyze as they move through, but note whether the thought is angry, excited, sad, or bored. As with noticing what time frame your thoughts exist in, this focus allows you to become aware of the dominant emotional qualities of the thoughts moving through your mind.

Meditative Visualization

Once you have established meditation as a habit, you can create the sensation of meditation for yourself in a moment simply by closing your eyes and visualizing yourself meditating and feeling the peace, harmony, and balance you experience when you are meditating. This is a very useful tool when you do not have the time or the opportunity to meditate.

This technique is particularly useful when you are approaching a situation that is stressful for you such as caring for a patient in extreme pain or walking into a staff meeting you know will be volatile. It is also a good way to make constructive use of your time when you are standing in line at the bank or supermarket.

SACRED PLACES

Places of worship or ritual, particularly those in which many people have prayed or meditated for an extended period of time, are saturated with the uplifting qualities of serenity and peacefulness. This could be a church, temple, mission, or spiritual monument. Sitting in meditation in such a sacred place provides an environment in which you can deepen your meditative practice. Taking refuge in your hospital's chapel or quiet room during the middle of a hectic day for even a few minutes of meditation can make a big difference in how the rest of your day proceeds.

GROUP MEDITATION

There is a synergy created when a group meditates together that is far greater than the sum of the individuals. When all the minds in a room are focused in meditation, there is an energy generated that brings the entire group to a deeper state of consciousness.

Group meditation can be particularly helpful as you are beginning your practice for it provides a structure and a discipline you may have difficulty establishing on your own. A variety of spiritual groups offer group meditations. These can range from as short as half an hour to several hours.

Group meditative retreats are also available. The length of retreat can vary from a few days to a few months. A retreat is a very powerful way to deepen your practice. As the effects of meditation are cumulative, the intensive experience of a retreat where you meditate for many hours each day can accelerate your growth tremendously. As was noted in chapter 3, recent research has shown that the greatest degree of psychological health was attained by meditators who had participated in a meditation retreat.

PORTABLE PEACE

Although it is important in developing the meditative habit to start with a specified time and place for your practice, the beauty of meditation is that it can be practiced anywhere at any time; it is truly portable peace. Even if you just have a few minutes' break, all you need do is find a quiet place, be it your car, the supply room, or even a stall in the rest room.

As you become more adept at mindfulness, you can meditate with your eyes open as you stand in line or walk down the street. With practice, your body develops a cellular memory of what the meditative state feels like. As this grows, you exist more and more in this state of awareness and experience everyday living as a meditation. Your presence, the peace and bliss you emanate, becomes a living blessing to your patients, coworkers, family, and friends.

Suggested Reading

Hanh, Thich Nhat. (1987). *Being peace.* Berkeley, CA: Parallax Press.

Harp, D. (1990). *The new three minute meditation.* Oakland, CA: New Harbinger Publications.

Kornfield, J., & Goldstein, J. (1987). *Seeking the heart of wisdom.* Boston: Shambhala Publications.

8 EXPERIENCES ALONG THE WAY

As you journey on the path, remain open but always move forward.

A TIME FOR EVERY PURPOSE UNDER HEAVEN

As you move along in your meditative process, you may have various experiences as you grow, develop, and unfold. This chapter will offer some insight regarding these experiences.

RUTS

There may be times in your journey when you feel as though nothing is happening either internally in your meditations or externally in your life. Meditators often refer to these times as dry spells or ruts. Sometimes it may even feel as though your meditations are less deep than they were the month before. For example, when you are sitting in meditation, you may have difficulty focusing, your mind may be scurrying from one thought to the next, and any feelings of peace or calmness are elusive. Do not despair; this happens occasionally to just about everyone.

If you are having one of these dry spells, try one or more of the deepening techniques described in chapter 7. Sometimes exercising aerobically or doing hatha yoga before your meditation may be useful as they give you a sense of motion. If nothing you try seems to help, just be patient and compassionate with yourself and know that this period will pass.

Even though it may appear otherwise, movement is still occurring during these periods. It may be unknown to you consciously, but it is always happening. The river is continually flowing, faster as it enters a narrow passageway, slower as it spreads out in the delta or flows around some large boulders.

Another useful way to look at the process of your growth is to contemplate the nature of a spiral. In its ever constant movement upward the spiral has periods when it is moving forward but appears to be on the same level as it was previously. Then it turns a corner, and suddenly it is on a higher level.

Or contemplate the process of a flower blooming. It appears externally that nothing is happening; the bud is sitting closed on its stem for quite some time. But the reality is that there is much occurring that cannot yet be seen. Then one day, when it is least expected, there is a small opening at the bud's center, and then little by little one petal after another unfolds until the flower has presented itself in its full glory.

BUMPS

Meditation moves you increasingly toward positive feelings such as calmness, harmony, and happiness and away from negative feelings of anxiety, anger, and depression. This movement at times is smooth, but at others it may feel a bit bumpy as deeply buried subconscious patterns surface to conscious awareness.

Surfacing the Subconscious

You might think of your consciousness as a soiled tablecloth. Originally, the tablecloth was fresh and clean. Over time, first one thing then another got spilled upon it until it has become covered with stains, one blending into the next. But now you have found a new spot remover, and every time you wash that tablecloth there are fewer stains. Now that there is space between the stains that had seemed to run one into the other, you can see the individual spots. Or you might relate this cleansing process to pulling weeds from your garden to provide the space and nutrients for your flowers to flourish.

These spots or weeds — long-buried subconscious feelings, thoughts, beliefs, and attitudes — now come into focus for you to look at them. Maybe a childhood memory bubbles up about how your mother told you you were not very bright. All of a sudden you realize how this belief has been with you all these years. Perhaps it has hindered you from advancing in your career, even though deep inside you know that you can successfully get that master's degree or that promotion you desire.

Or perhaps you had lied to an ex-boyfriend and now, seemingly out of nowhere, your feelings of guilt about your behavior those many years ago come to mind. Maybe you trusted someone who was not trustworthy, and now you find yourself feeling regretful for having done so. Or maybe a memory of a supervisor who had treated you unfairly comes up, and a new wave of anger toward her passes through your awareness.

These realizations may surface during your meditation as thoughts, feelings, or visual pictures. Or they may reveal themselves to you in dreams or as sudden flashes when you are in the midst of an unrelated activity.

Updating Your Reality

Everything that is a memory was a conscious thought at one point in time. These thoughts are moved into your subconscious storehouse, and, particularly if painful, they often remain repressed. These repressed memories, however, can inhibit your happiness and your growth for they take up space in your mind that could be used more productively. And, if they have to do with negative belief patterns — you are not good enough, smart enough, attractive enough, capable enough, and so forth — they can limit what you experience in your everyday life.

Meditation stimulates the movement of these outdated thoughts, beliefs, and attitudes that are no longer serving your best interests. The next step is to release the outdated to make way for the new. A biblical passage addresses this concept when it speaks to the idea of dying each day to be born again. As you let the old ideas die and release them, you create the space for the new ideas to become your current identity.

The Releasing Process

Sometimes an outdated belief or pattern will release spontaneously in an "aha" experience. Other times a limiting belief will disappear without it ever having come to your conscious awareness. For example, say you had a longstanding pattern of being afraid of authority figures. After meditating for a while, you find yourself meeting with the supervisor of your unit who previously terrified you, but you notice something is different in your interaction. Those usual feelings of fear and intimidation are no longer with you.

Tools and Guides to Assist You

There may be occasions, however, when particularly painful memories or pieces of a memory are revealed, and you have difficulty releasing them and moving on. Indications of this are when the hurt feelings seem to overwhelm you or you find your mind talking continuously to that person who was involved in the incident. Or you may have an unexplainable physical pain or an obsessive thought you cannot get rid of. These are all ways your consciousness is getting you to pay attention, making you a bit uncomfortable so that you will look at what needs to be addressed.

The bottom line in release work is forgiveness — forgiveness of the one who appeared to have harmed you, forgiveness of yourself for appearing to have harmed another, or forgiveness of yourself for having engaged in a relationship or activity that was not in your best interest. Specific ways for working with forgiveness in the journal writing process are presented in chapter 12.

You can often help yourself release through forgiveness exercises and affirmations. Affirmations are declarations of a positive nature. They work by bringing the future into the present time. Specific instructions on using affirmations for release and renewal work are presented in chapter 12.

Other times you may feel a need to access some assistance in the form of an insightful friend, a spiritual teacher or guide, or a spiritually oriented psychotherapist. It is a friendly universe, and the right resources do come to assist you when you ask. An affirmation for such assistance could be, "I know that the right resources to assist me with this stage of my growth are here for me now." Keep in mind, above all else, that whatever it is you are currently moving through it is temporary; it is of a transient nature just like the clouds that move in the sky. And when this passes, your tablecloth will be cleaner, your garden healthier.

SPECTACLES

Most people only use a very small portion of their minds, but the potential of the mind is virtually without limits. One of the many benefits of meditation is its ability to awaken capabilities of the mind heretofore untapped. As was noted in chapter 3, enhanced creativity is a frequently reported effect of meditation. Other experiences or expressions of expanded mind capabilities are also possible.

The theoretical framework the Hindus use to explain this process is the *chakra* system — a series of seven spinning energy wheels located along an energy pathway that extends from the base of the spine to the crown of the head. These energy centers are associated with specific endocrine glands and certain abilities that are considered extrasensory, or beyond the range of what is commonly experienced through the use of the five senses. Through meditation some or all of these centers may be stimulated.

This explains why some people during meditation may experience seeing lights of varying colors and intensities or visual pictures with their eyes closed. Others may hear unusual sounds or have extraordinary taste, smell, or kinesthetic sensations. Some experience increased remembrance of dreams or a change in the quality of their dreams.

If you experience any of these phenomena, it is important not to be frightened by them. At the same time it is just as important not to get caught in them, to become so fascinated or captivated by spectacles that you lose track of your reason for meditating, which is to grow into a more compassionate, loving, centered human being who is conscious of an ever deepening connection with God.

Expending your energy trying to re-create a phenomenon you experienced in one meditation diverts your attention from your growth in pure consciousness. Just accept the experience as any other you have had in your life and let it move into the past. Clinging to it keeps you from having your full attention in the present moment. Being present in the now is the essence of meditation and living meditatively.

Sometimes your meditations can present you with symbolic tools you can use for your psychological and spiritual growth. For example, a woman who had for years experienced severe depression and had attempted suicide a few times had a vision in her meditation of a golden baby floating through a tunnel covered in deep green foliage. In psychotherapy sessions prior to this meditation, the only images she could capture of herself were of a little girl hiding in a corner and a stick figure. Her realization from the meditative vision was that she was being reborn spiritually. Her suicide attempts, she recognized, had been efforts to destroy the unhealthy images of her self. What resulted for her was the understanding that the key to her healing was to build a new self from the inside out. The power of that meditative vision led her to rededicate herself to her practice, which had become a low priority in her life.

If you do not experience any phenomena, that is also fine. Not everyone does, and it is not the point of meditation. It does not mean that you are growing any slower than someone who is having such experiences. The same energy that may give one person a vision or prophetic dream may provide another with a spontaneous "aha" experience, whereas another may be gifted with the opening of new creative channels. Yet another may grow profoundly in her experience to love, and someone else may move into a sense of knowingness that is beyond words.

Be wary of judging with such thoughts as "my meditation experience is better or lesser than yours." What is yours is meant uniquely for you; what is for others is what they need for their next steps on their spiritual journeys. Remember, all is progress, and all is good.

Suggested Reading

Chinmoy, Sr. (1984). *Meditation: Man-perfection in god-satisfaction* (5th ed.). Jamaica, NY: Agni Press.

Kornfield, J. (1993). *A path with heart.* New York: Bantam.

Ram Daas. (1990). *Journey of awakening: A meditator's guidebook.* New York: Bantam.

2 JOURNAL WRITING

I open myself to allow my personal truth to flow forth.

9 | WRITING FOR YOURSELF

I write to know and to grow.

YOUR CHILDHOOD DIARY

Did you have a diary when you were in grade school? Maybe as a teenager? Was it the open type or did it have a little lock and key? If you did have a diary, it may have been your best friend at some point in your life. It was the place where you could safely write your secret thoughts and feelings, your deepest desires and dreams.

Your diary may have contained an account of what happened at school each day, your first crush, what your best friend said to you on the telephone, feelings — sad, glad, and in-between — or even something as mundane as what you had for dinner. But it was totally about you and what was important to you at that time. It was somewhere that no one else could go unless invited. It was off-limits to your younger brother and your older sister and definitely to your parents. It was written by you just for you.

YOUR ADULT JOURNAL

Keeping a journal as an adult is not unlike keeping a childhood diary, although you can choose at this point in your life to give a more directive focus to the content. This book is designed to provide you with opportunities to use what you write in your journal for the specific purposes of self-exploration and personal growth. It can be a self-monitoring tool and a way of finding or reawakening parts of your self currently unknown to you.

THE PROCESS OF WRITING

Letting It Flow

Many people did not have good experiences with writing when they were in school; as adults these beliefs can be inhibiting. The first step in freeing yourself to write is to let go of any unpleasant memories you may be carrying from your past. Journal writing is not like writing a term paper or an essay exam. Crossing the t's and dotting the i's does not matter.

You may feel that you cannot write because there is nothing inside you worth saying, or that you just do not know how to put what you are feeling or thinking onto paper. You may be a supernurse or an efficient administrator, but you just feel there is not a creative bone in your body.

Brenda Ueland, author of *If You Want to Write* (1987), makes an interesting recommendation for energetic, efficient people who feel they cannot write: ". . . they should be idle, limp and alone for much of the time, as lazy as men fishing on a levee, and quietly looking and thinking, not willing all the time. This quiet looking and thinking is the imagination; it is letting in ideas."

What Ueland is talking about here is being in an unstructured state of contemplative meditation — that place where the left brain, the "doing" brain, becomes quiet and the right brain, the "being" brain, becomes activated in the stillness.

Meditation Helps You Write

One of the wonderful benefits of meditation is that it allows more access to the intuitive, holistic, artistic right brain. The very practice of meditation that brings you an increased sense of harmony and well-being is at the same time subtly opening doorways to greater knowing.

As you may recall from earlier chapters, during meditation the brain moves from the faster beta waves associated with the doing state to the slower alpha waves associated with holistic thinking. Your daily meditations provide you with training in concentration and relaxation, both essential tools for allowing the writing that is within you to flow forth.

Content for journal writing is brought forth through your meditations. A recurring thought that passes through your meditation on a regular basis could serve as a focal point for a journal entry. Likewise, a previously subconscious behavior pattern, attitude, or belief that comes to your awareness, either during or between meditations, can provide you with a starting point for journal writing.

The quantity of remembered dreams frequently increases with the regular practice of meditation as your mind processes content that is surfacing. Dream images are often a way your subconscious communicates to you in a symbolic format. This, then, provides yet another avenue for self-discovery through journal writing.

PREPARING FOR A JOURNAL WRITING SESSION

Just as you prepare for a meditation, you will find that you will similarly access yourself more deeply if you prepare before you actually begin to write. It is wonderful to establish a ritual for yourself. Set aside time to write in your journal at least once a week, and create a peaceful environment where you will be undisturbed for a while.

If indoors, you may want to light a candle or incense, or put some inspirational music on before you start writing. Many people find being in nature assists them to move into a writing mode. Placing yourself by the ocean, in the mountains, or under a favorite tree may appeal to you.

Wherever you decide to write, take a few minutes to meditate, or if that is not possible, bring yourself into a centered consciousness by doing a meditative visualization. By being in this state of mind in a comfortable, peaceful environment, you create an atmosphere conducive to writing. Chapter 10 provides you with some ideas for focusing your writing, and chapter 11 outlines specific techniques you may want to use.

Reference

Ueland, B. (1987). *If you want to write*. St. Paul: Graywolf Press.

Suggested Reading

Goldberg, N. (1986). *Writing down the bones: Freeing the writer within.* Boston: Shambhala Publications.

Hughes, E. F. (1991). *Writing from the inner self.* New York: Harper Perennial.

Snow, K. (1989). *Writing yourself home: A woman's guided journey of self-discovery.* Berkeley, CA: Conari Press.

10 JOURNAL WRITING FOCUSES

In directing my attention, I gain greater clarity.

LOOKING WITHIN

Journal writing is an experience of introspection, of looking inside yourself. It can be used as a tool for monitoring your growth over a period of time. You may have insights about yourself or realizations about your interactions in the world, but they are with you for only a day or two. A few weeks later you may try to recall what at the time had seemed so important only to find that the memory is vague or gone.

Recording these insights and revelations in a journal allows you to capture this information, providing you with the opportunity to review the material at a later date. Keeping a journal is a valuable feedback tool for seeing how you change in consciousness as a result of your meditative practice.

Sometimes people become frustrated with their meditative practices, feeling that nothing is changing in their lives as a result of their new habits. Although some people experience dramatic changes within a short time period after initiating meditation, the more usual pattern is for the changes to occur in more subtle ways than you are used to acknowledging.

Shifts occur in consciousness before they manifest externally. This is why keeping a journal is so helpful in becoming aware of the positive, perhaps subtle, changes you are experiencing in your awareness.

Even when you appear to be stuck in a rut with your meditations, writing in your journal can be a good way to vent any feelings of frustration or discouragement. You will find in looking back over your writings from a longer perspective that, even with the dry spells, you have moved quite a distance from where you started.

Your journal can be a self-monitoring tool, as well as a tool for self-exploration and discovery. As subconscious material bubbles to the surface through your meditations, dreams, and "aha" experiences, you can use your journal to find out more about who you are, develop new aspects of yourself, and release outdated beliefs and patterns that no longer benefit you.

SELECTING FOCUSES

There are a variety of ways you can direct your attention when journal writing, a few of which will be presented in this chapter. You may choose to use one or more of the focuses described here, or you may want to create your own personal way of being with your journal. Chapter 11 will present a variety of techniques that can be used with any selected focus.

Recording Observations, Insights, and Revelations

Perhaps the most straightforward approach to writing in your journal is to record observations, insights, and revelations regarding your interaction with yourself and with others. This may be pursued in a general manner in which you record at random whatever catches your attention, or you might pick an area of your life you are particularly interested in and focus your observations and recordings on that area. Figure 10.1 presents a series of possible journal entries concerning the area of romantic relationship.

Looking at these journal writings in retrospect can provide some interesting insights for the person who made these entries. She can see, for example, how her anger initially blocked her from making any movement in her relationship. Then she expands her consciousness a little and comes to some understanding about why she is afraid to confront her boyfriend. From there she looks at her victim attitude and

**FIGURE 10.1
Sample Journal
Entries**

2/5	Jim showed up two hours late for our date without calling beforehand to let me know. I was so furious that I couldn't even listen to his explanation, and we were both tense all evening.
3/6	He did it again! Showed up late without calling. I'm beginning to wonder why I'm letting Jim do this to me. It makes me so mad, but I'm afraid I'll lose him if I confront him.
4/11	Jim was late again, and again I didn't say anything. I think I'm as mad at myself for not talking to him as I am at him for doing what he is doing. Do I enjoy being a victim?
5/28	I almost got up the courage to talk to Jim tonight about his being late. The words were on the tip of my tongue a couple of times, but I just couldn't get them out.
7/22	I did it! Even though I was afraid that it would end our relationship, I made Jim sit down and talk with me about his habit of being late and not notifying me. He was as uncomfortable as I was in talking about it. But finally we were both able to talk about our feelings honestly. He asked me to forgive him, and promised to change his bad habit. I realize I need to forgive myself for letting myself play victim for so long. Something has shifted in our relationship — not sure what it is yet — but it feels better than before.

then to a stage of "almost." When she finally confronts her boyfriend, you can feel her excitement with both her action and the realization that results from her action.

Without the recording of these observations, the subtle movement from shifts in consciousness to changes in behavior may have gone unnoticed. Also, in observing your own particular pattern of interaction and the ways in which you move to resolve uncomfortable situations, you come to understand yourself better.

You can also transfer the insights gained from the analysis of your journal entries to other areas of your life. For example, if you are codependent and not expressing yourself honestly in a romantic relationship, you may become aware that you are acting the same way on your job and with your friends. The exciting thing is that when you shift your consciousness in one area of your life, you can embody that new awareness and bring it into all areas.

Contemplative Focus

This way of working with your writing uses the meditative technique of contemplation as a focusing tool for generating information to record in your journal. This may be done in either a structured or unstructured way.

In part 3, the short statements included in each week's two-page spread provide material for a structured contemplation. The way to work with any of these statements, or any other inspired writing you choose, is to read it a couple of times, then close your eyes, take it inside in meditation, and be with it.

For example, suppose you are in the week that has the statement, "It is only when you empty yourself that you can experience the fullness of life." Just let your mind wander around that statement for a while. Be with the concept and let it be with you. Stay with it for at least 5 minutes. When you open your eyes, begin writing anything that comes to mind regarding that statement. Do not stop to think about the right word or punctuation, but instead let whatever is in your mind come forth in an uninhibited stream of consciousness. If nothing comes for you, there are some techniques in chapter 11 that may assist you in working with this type of focus.

Another avenue for a contemplative focus is a more unstructured approach. Here, as Thoreau described, you would sit quietly in a natural setting and contemplate what is around you. You might decide to set your attention on one object such as a nearby tree or expand your focus to include everything around you. Simply sit in quiet reverie, enjoying your surroundings and noticing what you are seeing and how you are feeling about it. Do not rush yourself. Sit for 15 minutes, half an hour, half a´day. When you feel complete, let whatever is moving through you flow through your pen and into your journal.

Meditative Material

As was discussed in chapter 8, meditation can bring long-buried subconscious material to the attention of the conscious mind. Journal writing is a way of exploring what comes to the surface.

For example, suppose you notice that you keep having thoughts come into your meditation regarding financial security. Using one or more of the techniques in chapter 11, you can explore this thought. You may be able to get underneath the thought to the feeling behind it and then perhaps to your personal experiences that created the feeling. This recurring thought could turn out to be a magnificent teacher to assist you in uncovering beliefs and releasing memories that no longer serve you.

Dreams

Another way subconscious material gets released is through dreams. As mentioned previously, meditators often notice that not only do the quantity of their dreams increase, but the quality of their dreams become richer and more informative as a result of regular meditative practice.

There are many kinds of dreams. Some are simply releasing data from an overloaded nervous system. Others are symbolic messages from your psyche asking you to pay attention to something that has not been in your conscious awareness; still others may be prophetic.

Some may repeat themselves periodically and be related to your individual growth cycle. For example, you may have a recurring dream about not having enough credits to graduate college even though you were sure you had more than enough. If you are recording your dreams in a journal, you may notice over time that this dream typically occurs when you are about to make a major life transition — change jobs, meet your mate, leave your mate, move to a new city, and so forth. Becoming cognizant of a dream pattern such as this may help you to be better prepared for these transitions.

Many books on dreams and dream symbols are available. These can help you understand what your dreams are communicating to you. Using these types of references and the tools in chapter 11, you can explore the nature of your nocturnal messages in your journal.

Suggested Reading

Faraday, A. (1972). *Dream power*. New York: Coward, McCann & Geoghegan, Inc.

Johnson, D. (1989). *Creative guide to journal writing: How to enrich your life with a written journal*. Louisville, CO: Gateway Publications.

Progoff, I. (1975). *At a journal workshop: The basic text and guide for using the intensive journal*. New York: Dialogue House Library.

Robinson, S., & Corbett, T. (1984). *The dreamer's dictionary*. London: Treasure Press.

11 | JOURNAL WRITING
TECHNIQUES

Having the right tools always makes the job easier.

CONNECTING THE INNER AND OUTER

Writing is a way of connecting your inner and outer worlds. Writing in a journal, regardless of the technique you select, provides you with a vehicle for taking a deeper look at what you experience externally. As you record and work with the events and interactions in your world, you come to understand your inner self in a new way. And as you contemplate meditatively or internal subconscious material comes to your conscious awareness, journal writing can provide you with the opportunity to see how your internal state of mind mirrors itself in your daily experiences.

QUIETING UNWANTED VOICES

Putting the Critic to Sleep

Everyone has an internal critic, that part of themselves who likes to say things such as, "You do not know how to do this," "What you are doing is not quite good enough," "You will never get it right," "You have never been good at expressing yourself," and so forth. You may be able to link this critic to people who were prominent in your early childhood — a parent, a teacher, or a sibling. Or your critic may have been activated later by an unsupportive spouse, a denigrating supervisor, or unfulfilling work experiences or personal relationships.

The critic has a tendency to get involved in your business when you are a little unsure of yourself. Your true self decides to engage in a new activity, one that will lead to personal growth, and your critic wakes up and sends your mind doubt messages.

But you do not have to let the critic get in your way. When your critic whispers in your ear, make an affirmative statement to the contrary. For example, if your critic starts talking to you as you are sitting down to write and says something such as, "You have nothing to write about," simply make an affirmative statement such as, "I am filled with wonderful ideas and insights, and I write them easily and effortlessly."

Your critic does not like these kinds of statements. Usually, with a little repetition of your affirmation, you will find that he will go back to sleep. But if for some reason your critic is very tenacious, you might want to visualize him with a feather growing out of his left ear or skating backward blindfolded and then repeat your affirmation a few more times.

Setting the Editor Aside

Writing involves both the right and left sides of the brain. The inspiration, the ideas, the flowing of thoughts emanates from the right brain — the artist. The left brain — the editor — is responsible for the structure, the grammar, the logical sequencing of thoughts. Both sides are important in creating a piece of writing that is at the same time inspirational and understandable.

With journal writing, it is important to set the editor aside. Journal writing is more a right brain activity than a left one. It is a tool for accessing the intuitive, creative, knowing side of your brain. Its content is designed to be understood by one person and one person only — you.

The left brain editor in you should be ignored when you are writing in your journal. Grammar rules, correct spelling, preciseness, and logical sequencing of ideas do not matter in this type of writing. What is important is allowing the intuitive mind to come to the surface. The following techniques are designed to assist you in this accessing process.

FLOW WRITING

One technique to use for journal writing is flow writing. This style is also known as stream of consciousness writing or rapid writing. It is actually quite a simple technique. You place your pen on your journal page and write whatever comes through you. Do not stop to read it. Just write until you feel finished. Even if it makes no sense to you, your critic is calling it garbage, or your editor is getting fidgety, just let it flow onto the page.

Some proponents of this writing technique suggest that you write immediately upon arising, before having a morning coffee or thinking about what activities will fill your day. In that state between sleep and full wakefulness is an opening for what has surfaced from the previous night.

You can use this technique in two ways: starting without a focus for the writing or with one. If you begin without a focus for your writing, one or more focal points may present themselves to you when you read what you have written. You might want to work with these areas through dialogue or mindmapping techniques, which are presented later in this chapter.

There may be times, however, when what you have just written makes no sense to you at all. This is all right. You might draw an analogy to the cleaning of a clogged pipe. First, the debris needs to be released, then the way is cleared for the flow to begin. Make sure your critic is asleep; do not judge yourself. Let what is be, knowing that you are exercising a muscle that may not have been used for quite some time.

This technique may also be used when you have established a focus for your journal writing, be it contemplating spiritual thoughts or qualities, working with material that has surfaced from your meditations, or looking at your dreams. Establish your focus, and then let the writing flow unedited but directed toward your chosen focal point.

WRITING WITH YOUR NONDOMINANT HAND

What should you do if you sit down to do flow writing and nothing flows? There you are poised with your pen on the page, and there you sit and continue to sit with your pen resting unmoving on the paper — no thoughts, no feelings, no words. A technique that may assist you here is to place your pen in your nondominant hand. This is a way to shift yourself out of your usual operating mode and open to your intuitive self.

With the pen in your nondominant hand, start making some simple open circles for a few minutes. Then switch the pen to your dominant hand and allow your rapid writing to begin. If nothing is moving for you, write a silly sentence or two with your nondominant hand. For example, you might write something such as, "The cat licked the dog's ear for dessert." Again, place the pen back in your dominant hand and begin writing.

Researchers have also found that writing with the nondominant hand directly accesses the right brain of the inner child (Foster, 1993). By switching between the dominant and nondominant hands, you can establish a written dialogue between your inner child and your adult. Using dialogue as a journal writing technique is discussed in the next section.

DIALOGUE

Dialogue with yourself or aspects of your self is another useful technique that can be used with any selected focus. For example, say you decide to contemplate the quality of joy as the focus of your journal writing. A possible dialogue that might evolve is presented in figure 11.1.

If your critic is trying to get in your way when you sit down to write, you might want to engage it in a dialogue such as the one presented in figure 11.2.

Suppose you are applying for a supervisor position. In general you feel confident, but there is something inside you that is a little fearful. You may want to allow a dialogue through journal writing with your dominant and nondominant hands. Let your adult dominant hand

FIGURE 11.1 Sample Self-Dialogue

Q. What is the nature of joy?
A. An emotion, or maybe a state of being.
Q. Which one — an emotion or a state of being?
A. If it is an emotion, joy could be a response to something happening in the external world.
Q. Then joy comes and goes depending on what is happening in your life?
A. Well, I have had that experience of feeling joyful when everything is going my way and not joyful when things are not the way I want them to be.
Q. But I have seen people who remain in a state of joy regardless of what is going on in their lives.
A. Well, then maybe joy can be both an emotion and a state of being.

FIGURE 11.2
Sample Critic
Dialogue

You:	Critic, why are you talking to me?
Critic:	I am concerned about you.
You:	Concerned about what?
Critic:	That you not make a fool of yourself.
You:	How would I make a fool out of myself?
Critic:	You do not know how to write. Remember how you barely got through your English classes?
You:	Yes, I remember that.
Critic:	Well, why do you want to embarrass yourself again?
You:	I don't care about embarrassing myself; I just want to find out more about myself. Besides, the only person who is going to read this is me.
Critic:	But you already know yourself.
You:	Not the way I want to.
Critic:	Oh, you foolish, foolish child.
You:	I am not a foolish child. I am a mature adult now, and I am seeking my own wisdom, not yours. And I *will* write and learn what I need to learn.

ask your inner child nondominant hand to communicate about the fear. This is a very useful tool for clarifying emotions that do not make sense to your adult self.

MINDMAPPING

Mindmapping is a whole brain approach to presenting information developed by Tony Buzan and described in his book *Use Both Sides of Your Brain* (1974). Whereas presenting information in an outline form relies on the linear, sequential left brain, mindmapping provides an opportunity for the right brain to become involved in a visual way. The result is a process that is conducive to creative thinking, and one that is particularly useful as a journal writing technique. The mindmapping steps are:

- Place a central focus of a visual image or a single printed word in a circle in the center of the page.

- Allow your ideas to flow freely without judgment.

- Use one printed key word to represent each idea.

- Connect each key word with a line to the central focus.

- To develop each key word, add branches to those lines.

• Color, images, and symbols may be used to highlight and to stimulate further generation of ideas.

If for your journal focus you were contemplating the statement, "Plant your seeds and nurture them with love and right action," you might develop a mindmap in your journal that looks like figure 11.3.

Mindmapping is also a very useful technique for working with your dreams, especially when your dreams are talking to you in a sym-

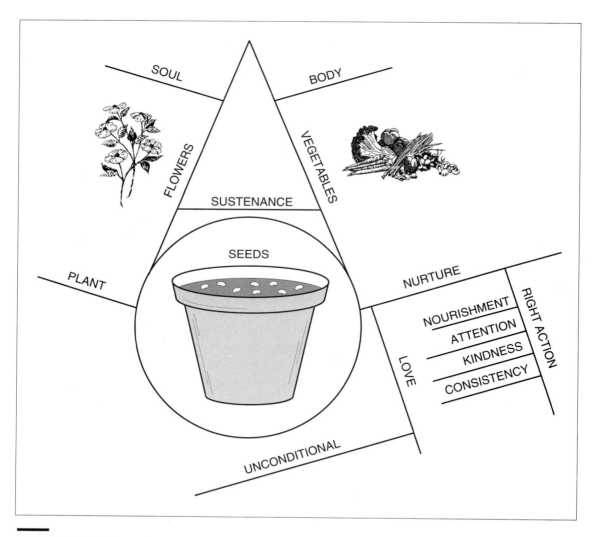

FIGURE 11.3   Sample Contemplation Mindmap

bolic format. If you had a dream where all you remember is that you were climbing up an unsupported ladder, place the ladder in the center of your mindmap and let your mind freely associate. A possible mindmap could look like the one in figure 11.4.

One way to analyze dreams is to look at each element or character in the dream as an aspect of yourself. A mindmap could be helpful in assisting you in this process, particularly if the dream was complex and you had no inkling as to its meaning. In this situation, you would take each character or element and place it in the center of a separate page, and let your map branch out from the central idea or image. Once you have done them all, place the individual sheets before you and let yourself contemplate the images and words. Allow the insights and revelations to come to you.

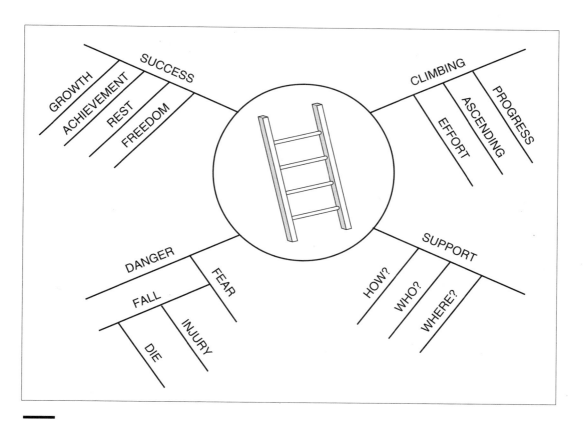

FIGURE 11.4   Sample Dream Mindmap

Mindmapping can also be used as a starting point for flow writing or dialogue. The mindmap may clarify the issue or bring it into sharper focus for you. You then may feel moved to rapid write or dialogue as a means for moving yourself deeper.

References

Buzan, T. (1974). *Use both sides of your brain.* New York: E. P. Dutton, Inc.

Foster, C. (1993). *The family patterns workbook.* New York: Putnam.

Suggested Reading

Cameron, J. (1992). *The artist's way: A spiritual path to higher creativity.* Los Angeles: Jeremy P. Tarcher.

Klauser, H. (1987). *Writing on both sides of the brain.* New York: HarperCollins.

Wycoff, J. (1991). *Mindmapping: Your personal guide to exploring creativity and problem-solving.* New York: Berkley Books.

Chapter

12

RELEASE AND RENEWAL

A new opening into a larger reality awaits you.

POWERFUL TOOLS

Meditation and journal writing are each independently powerful self-discovery tools. In the previous pages you have been provided guidance on how to work with each of these tools. Now, in this final chapter, you will be presented with a perspective on how to use the two together for release and renewal.

JOURNAL WRITING SURFACED MATERIAL

As was discussed in chapter 8, meditation can be an effective psychotherapeutic process. This process should be welcomed, not feared. As you release your previously buried limitations, you actually create space for more fulfillment and happiness in your life.

Subconscious material that surfaces through meditation can be used as a focal point for your journal writing. You may choose to work with the material using flow writing, mindmapping, dialogue, or any other technique that interests you.

Whatever technique you choose, your intent should be to get to the central idea or core issue. For example, suppose during a meditation or a dream you catch bits of an image of some scenes involving you and your mother during your early childhood. When you first look at what is being presented to you, the message is not at all clear.

To work with this material, take a few deep breaths, close your eyes, and take the images inside. As you revisit the images, make an affirmative statement such as, "I am being shown the core issue behind these images." Repeat this statement, either aloud or internally, at least 3 times. Open your eyes and start writing in your journal. If nothing comes, try your nondominant hand to access your inner child, or dialogue between your dominant hand and nondominant hand. If still nothing presents itself to you, record the images in your journal and set it aside.

When you do not have an insight at the time you seek it, it is usually because you are not ready to process the surfaced material. Simply release the images. If there is something important in these images for your growth and understanding, it will come to you at a later time.

WORKING WITH FORGIVENESS

Feelings of hurt, anger, resentment, and betrayal are not uncommon when long-buried memories of unresolved relationships come to the foreground. These memories need to be released with forgiveness, for it is only in fully forgiving that you release yourself completely from the emotional turmoil of the memory. This forgiveness release work is twofold. First, the people who appeared to have wronged you need to be forgiven, and secondly, you need to forgive yourself for having needed to participate in those experiences.

In moving into this atmosphere of forgiveness, it is very useful to look a little deeper. It is important to come to the realization that everything, everyone, and every experience in your life serves a purpose. Continuous learning is the true richness of living. What you have experienced, regardless of how painful it may have been for you, is the unique way in which you have chosen to learn. In taking responsibility for your actions, the process of forgiveness and release becomes easier.

And once you release, you will find that you are filled with new energy. You can actually physically feel how much energy had been trapped, unable to be expressed with these old emotions. Once freed, you move forward lighter and more optimistic.

Journal Writing for Release

Once you identify the experience you want to release and the people involved in that experience, take a few steps back and move into a space of compassion. Let yourself feel deep sympathy and a desire to alleviate the suffering involved in the experience. If feelings of anger, resentment, or unwillingness to release come up, just be with them until they pass. Then move yourself back into a feeling of compassion. When you have some sense of compassion — you certainly do not need to be fully immersed in it — you are ready to start your journal writing.

Set your intention before you begin writing with an affirmative statement such as, "I intend to release any negative feelings regarding this experience and the people involved in it, including negative feelings I am holding toward myself." Then begin flow writing starting with the phrase, "I forgive." Figure 12.1 provides you with an example of such a journal entry.

Once you complete your writing, close your eyes and take a few long, deep breaths. Visualize yourself releasing the situation; feel it moving out of your body, out of your consciousness, out of your life. You should feel lighter after doing this. If not, read what you have written and do the visualization repeatedly until you do feel that the release has taken place. Do not be concerned if it takes you a few days or even weeks to reach this state. Hurts that run deep can take a little while to heal. Above all, be compassionate and nurturing with yourself.

FIGURE 12.1
Journal Writing
for Release

I forgive my supervisor, Mary, for her attempts to manipulate and control me. I know that Mary is doing the best she is capable of doing and being the best she is capable of being when she attempts to limit me. I know that she, like me, is learning how to trust herself and the universe more fully.

I forgive myself for not seeing the situation clearly and for letting myself get angry and resentful toward Mary. I forgive myself for not having the courage to speak to her directly. I know now that I have been doing the best I was able to with my incomplete understanding.

I now release any negative emotions toward Mary and myself and accept my willingness to speak with her from a space of compassion and unconditional love.

Affirmative Meditation for Release

Another way to work with the release process in conjunction with your journal writing work is through affirmative mantra meditation. A sample mantra meditation for the situation in figure 12.1 is, "I forgive Mary and myself and release the experience fully now."

From here you want to move into a reframing of who you are in relation to who you were when you were involved in an unhealthy relationship. This also can be accomplished through the use of affirmative mantra. A sample affirmation for the person in figure 12.1 is, "I am courageous and communicate compassionately."

Affirmations work by repetition. They create a new groove in the subconscious mind, replacing outdated thought forms. In addition to repeating your affirmative mantra during meditation, you may also want to make note cards with your two affirmations printed on them — one releasing the old situation and the second stating the new one. Place the cards in places where you will continuously see them — on the refrigerator, the mirror, the closet door, and so forth. The visual stimuli reinforce your meditations. Continue this process until you feel that any old feelings have been totally dissolved and you really believe the statement affirming your new reality.

CREATING YOUR OWN WAY

You now have in your possession two invaluable tools for personal growth and self-exploration — meditation and journal writing. Think of these tools as your friends, supportive guides who are with you to serve as wayshowers.

These friends will help you open new windows of knowledge and happiness. Your empty journal awaits you. Create something new, something truly magnificent for yourself in these pages. And remember, the universe is only awaiting your intention to grow to reveal more of its wonders to you.

Intention to Grow: How HT the wayshower to new windows of knowledge and happiness

3 | PERSONAL JOURNAL PAGES

In writing I explore my uniqueness and my place in the universe.

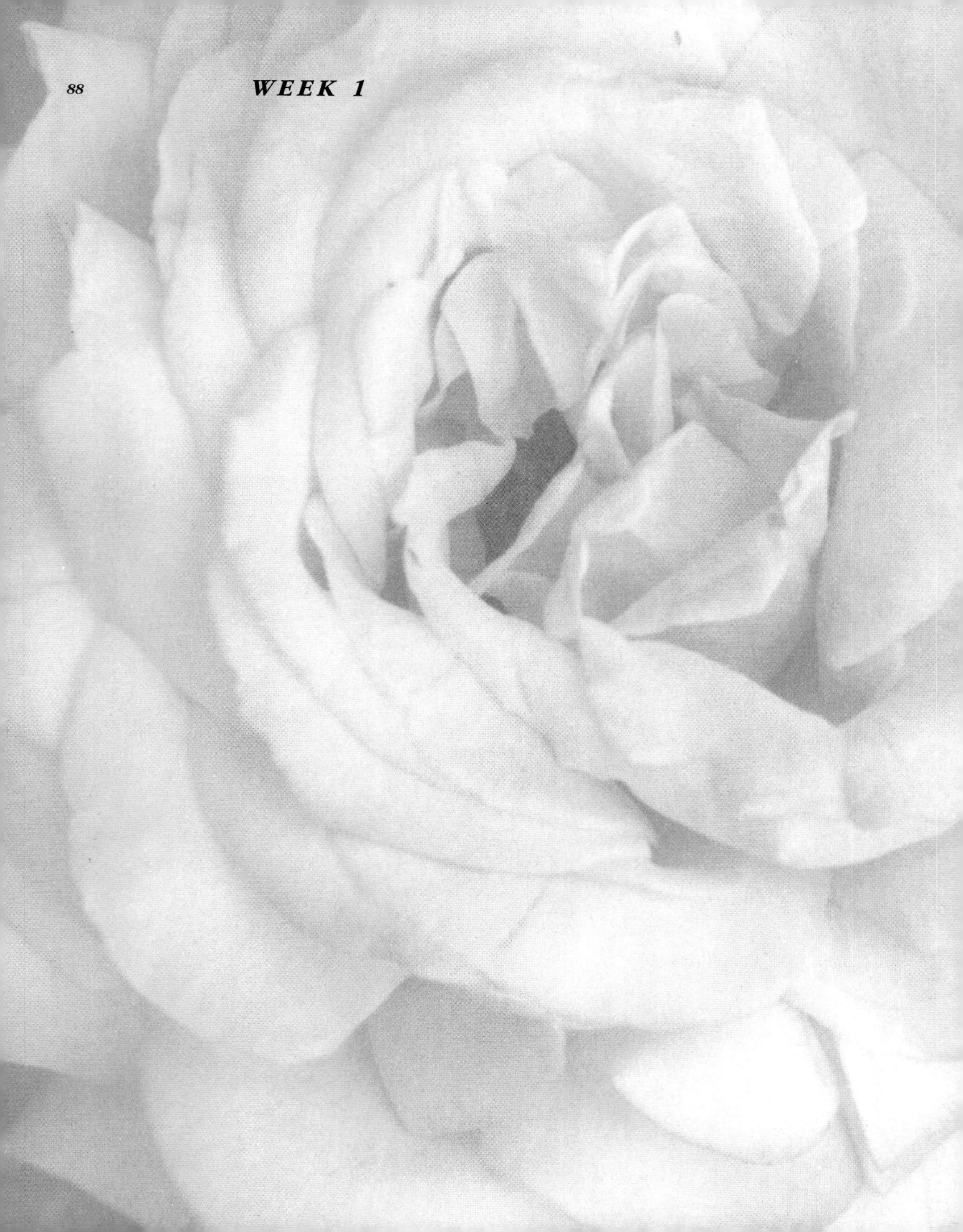

The only thing that is constant is change.

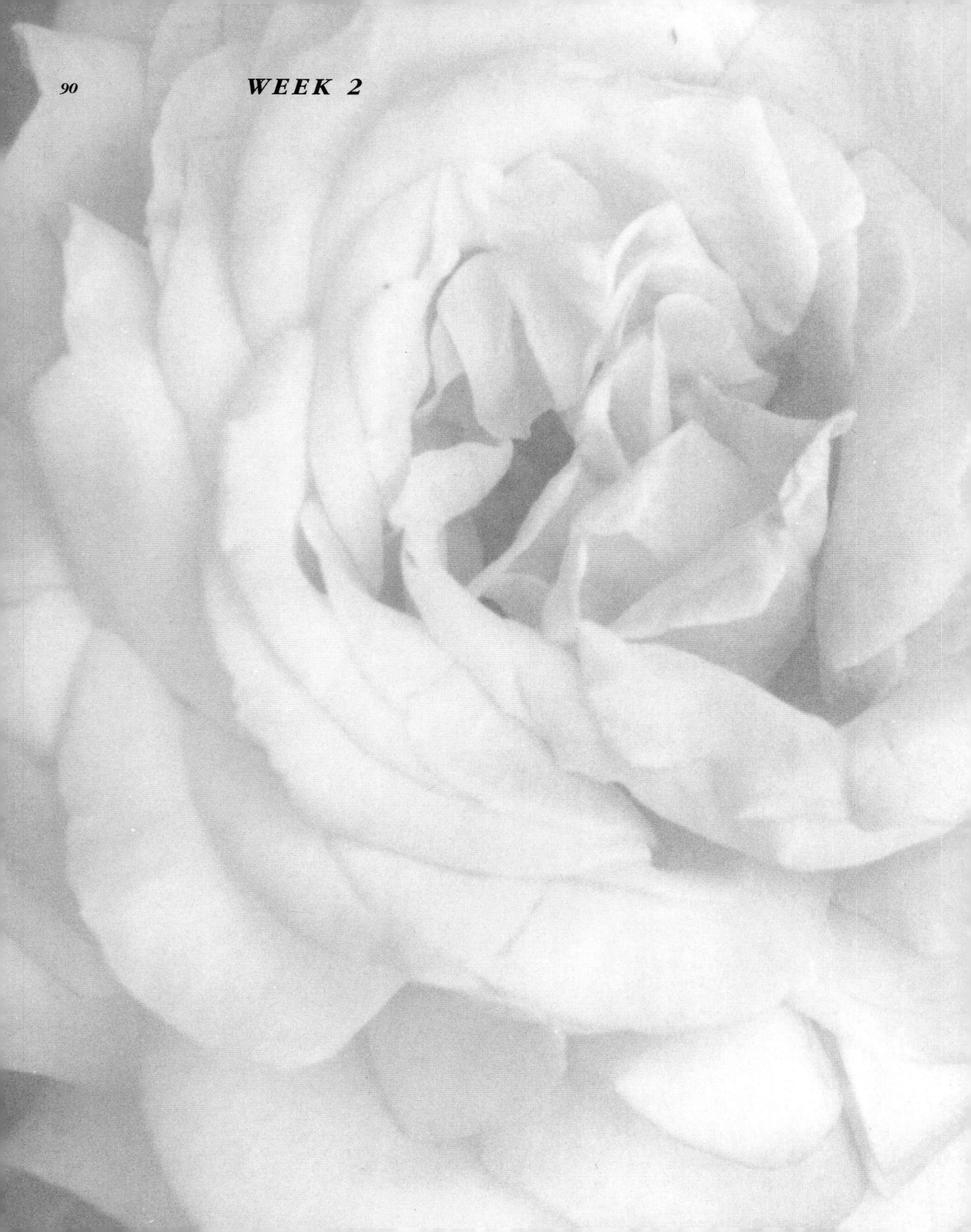

It is only when you empty yourself that you can experience the fullness of life.

Perception is a direct reflection of awareness.

*You attract to you what is in your thought atmosphere. To change
your circumstances, change your thoughts.*

When you ask, make sure your heart is pure and your intention is clear.

Nothing in the external world will bring you lasting happiness; all you need is within you.

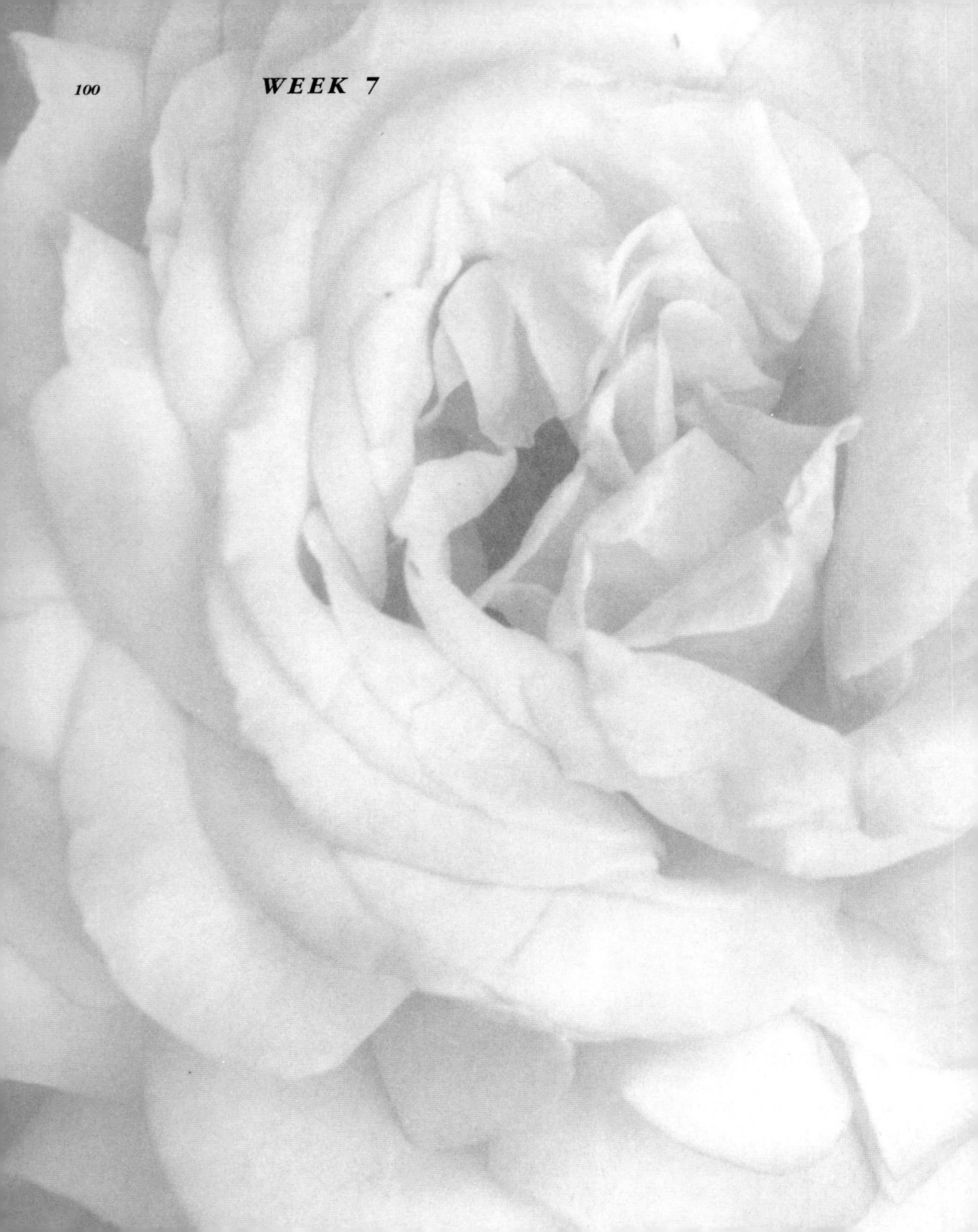

Anything you can imagine is possible, for if it did not exist you would not be able to imagine it.

WEEK 8

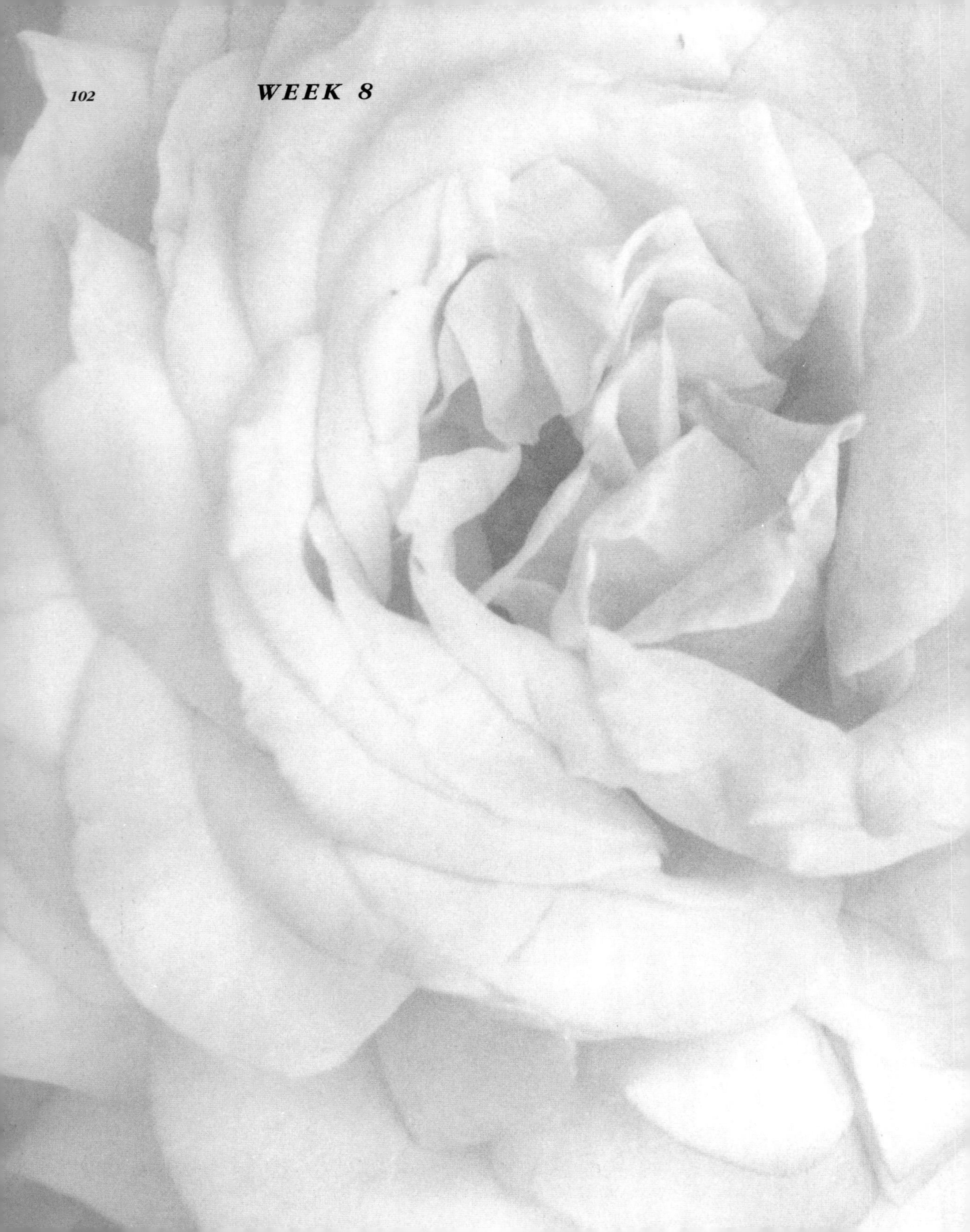

Do not be fearful of emptying yourself of that which is no longer you.
The universe always fills vacuums with that which you now are.

WEEK 9

You cannot be one way in one area of your life and different in others. There is only one life.

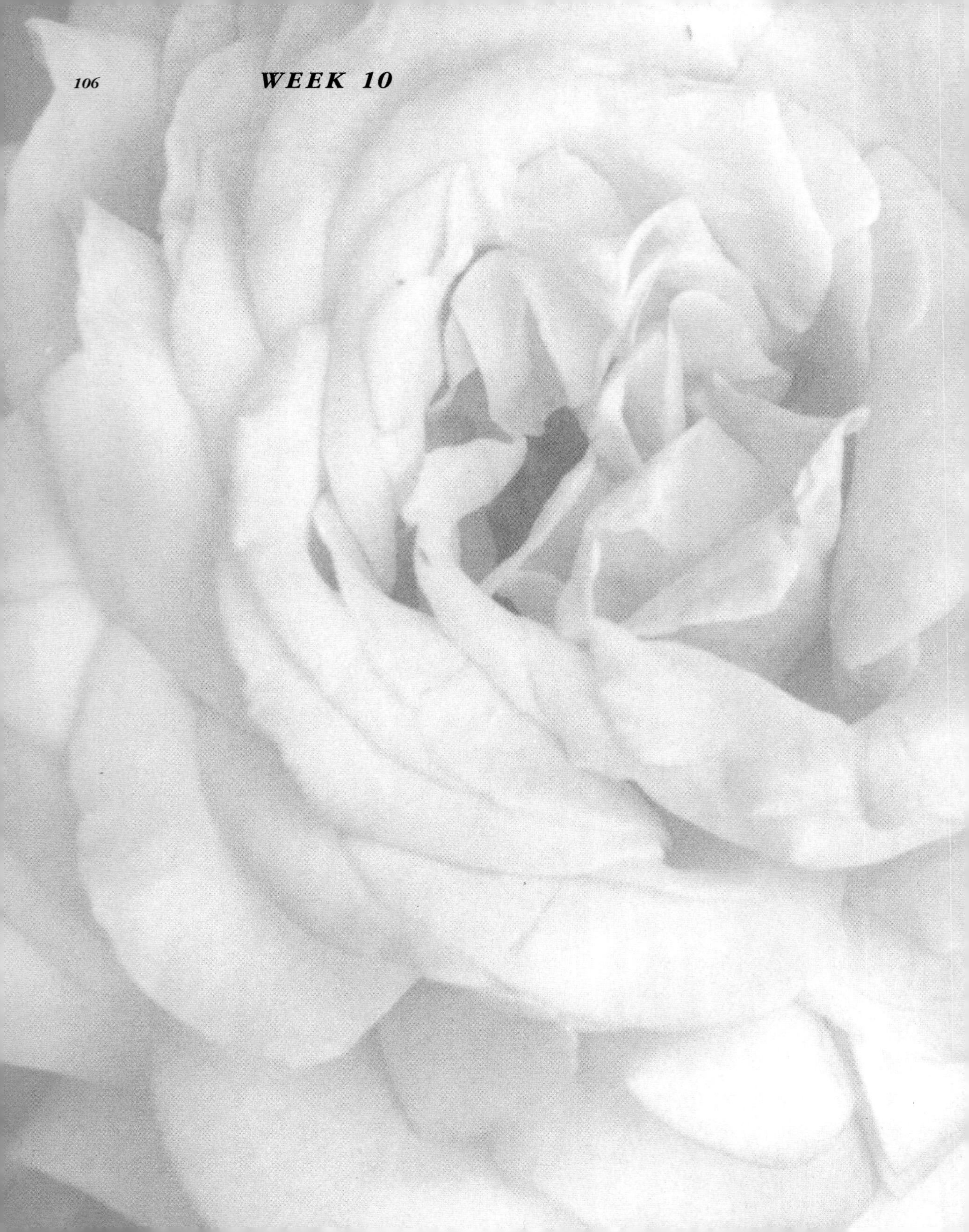

You are one leaf on the tree of life, unique unto yourself, but nourished continuously and infinitely by that which feeds the tree and all other leaves.

There is no place other than here and no time other than now; to be fully alive is to be here now.

Consciousness grows like the rose that unfolds petal by petal culminating in the revelation of its full beauty.

The way out is the way in.

To understand the natural rhythm that is you, watch nature and how she changes from season to season — germinating, blooming, and shedding only to begin the cycle once again.

When you know all is well, all is well despite external appearances.

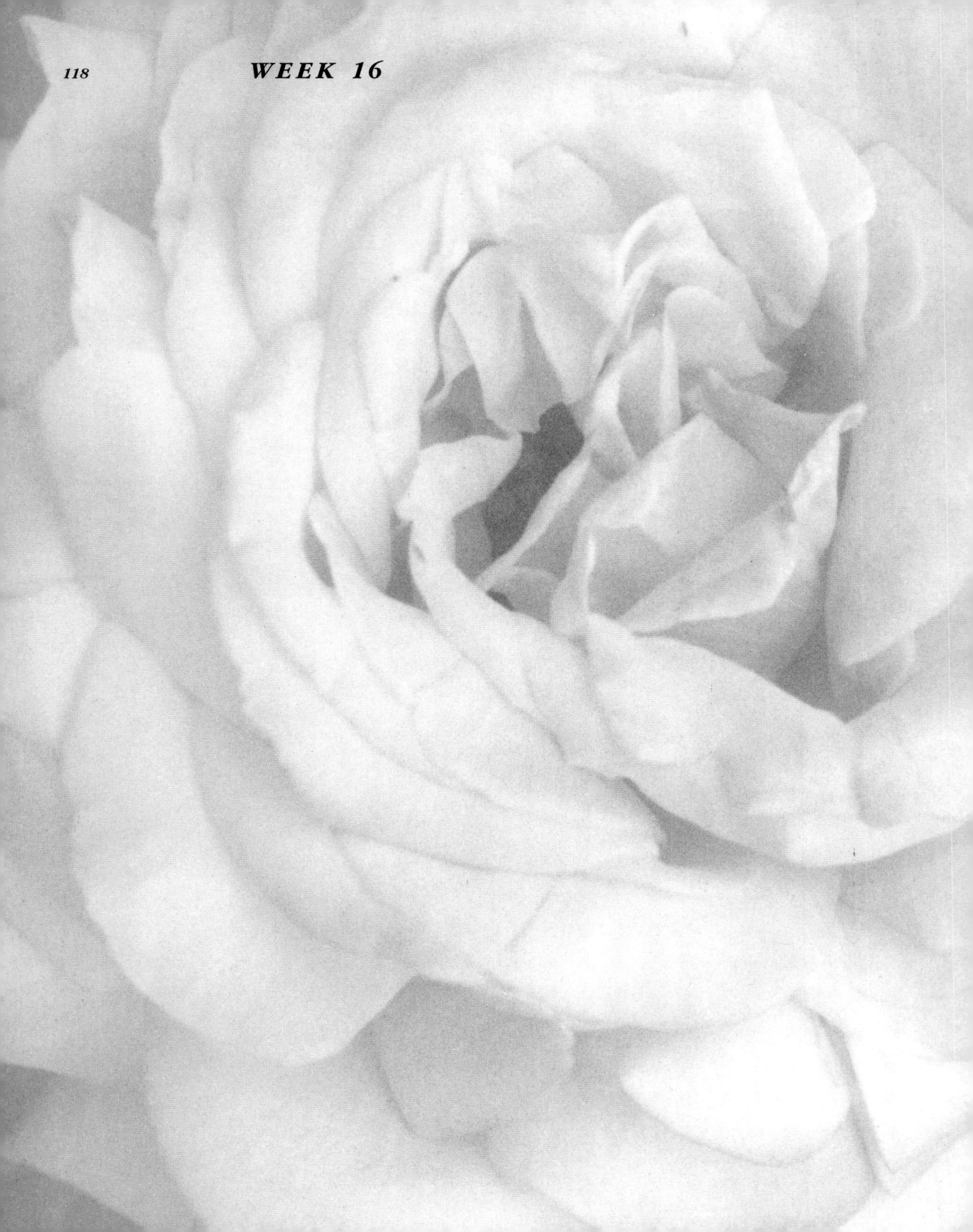

Eyes are mirrors of the soul — his-story/her-story untold.

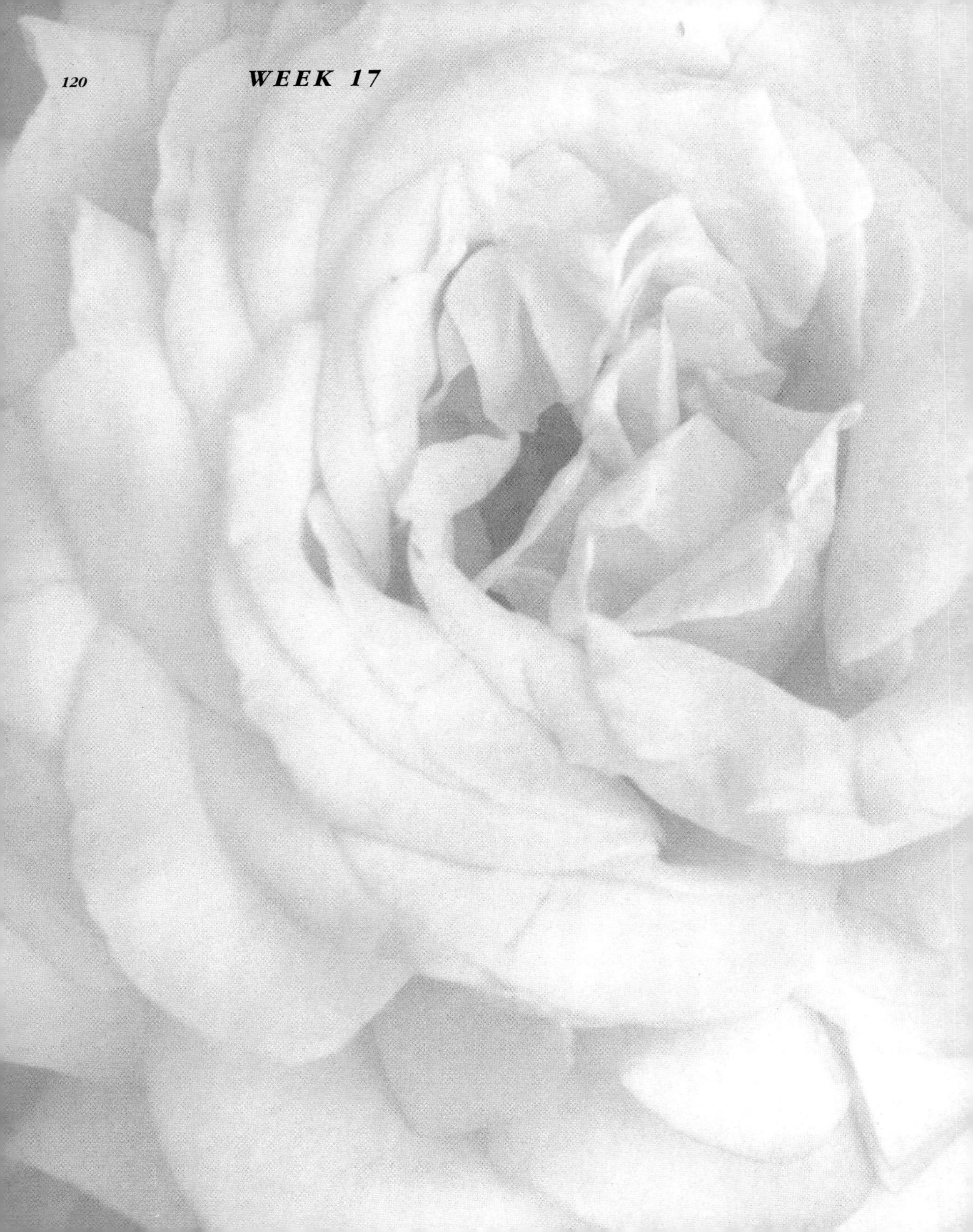

Live with the innocence of a child and the consciousness of a saint.

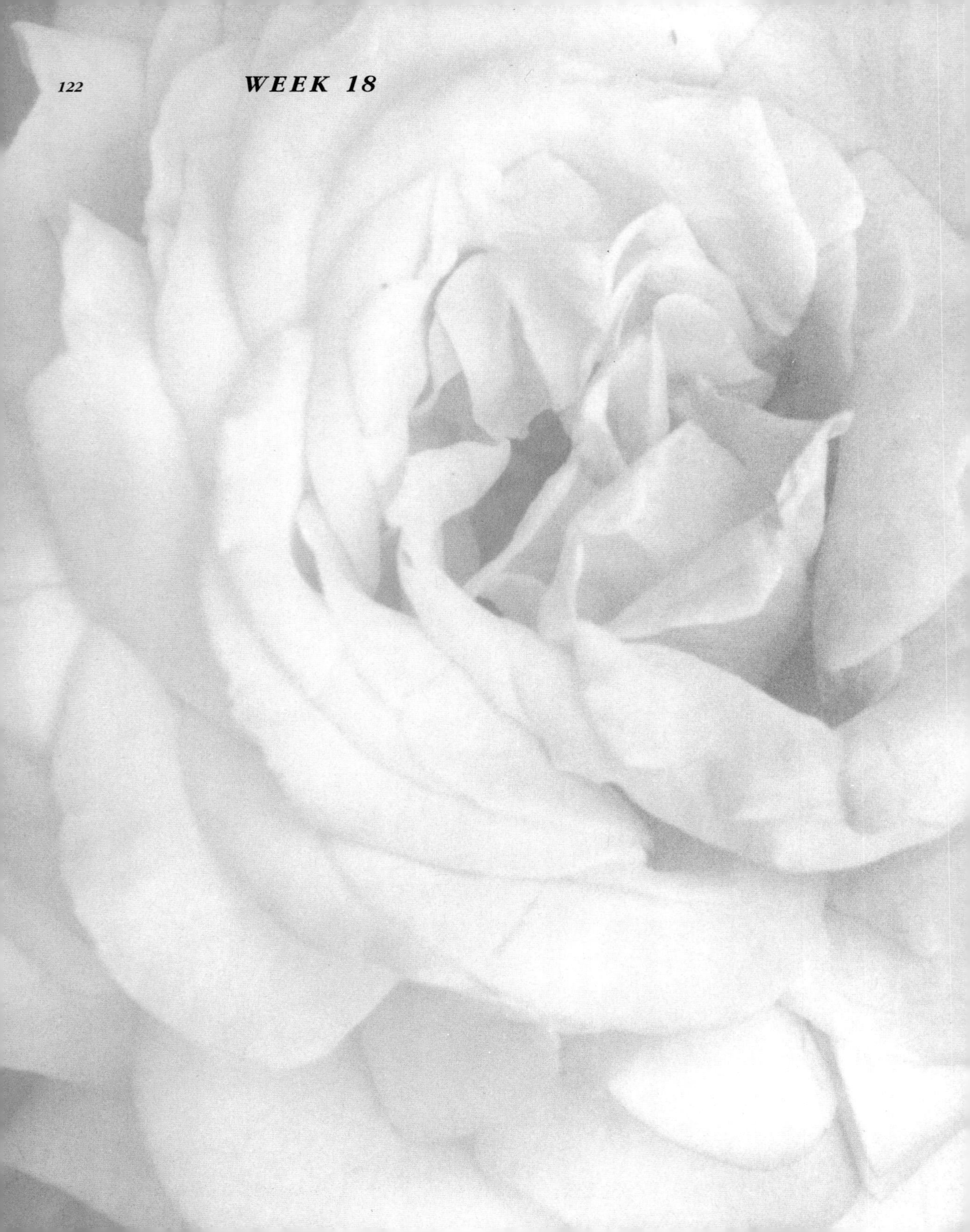

Plant your seeds and nurture them with love and right action.

WEEK 19

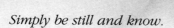

Simply be still and know.

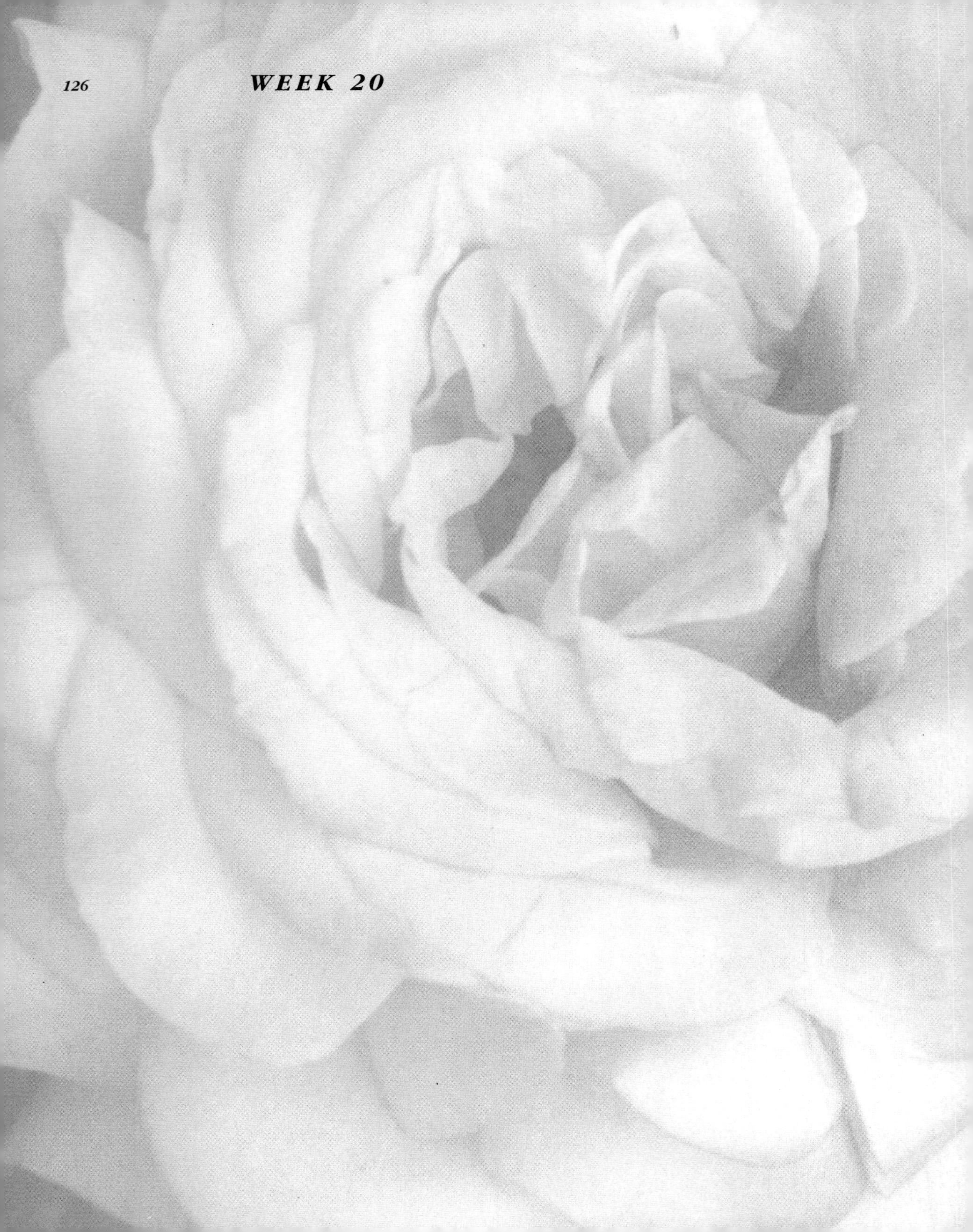

The only way to get there is to put one foot in front of the other.

Your body is a component of your consciousness; your consciousness is not a component of your body.

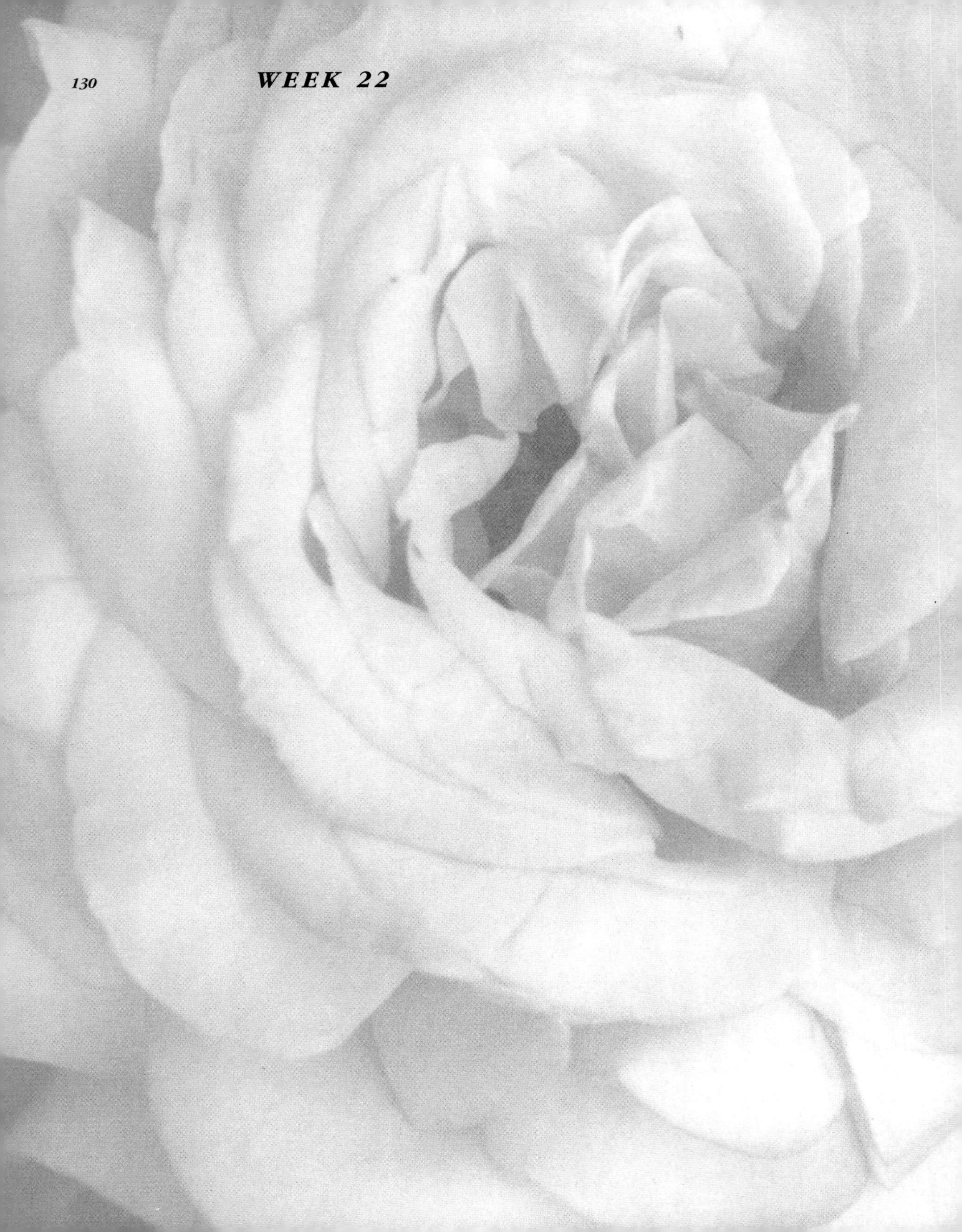

A rainbow is a perfect demonstration of unity in diversity.

WEEK 23

At the very center is pure silence.

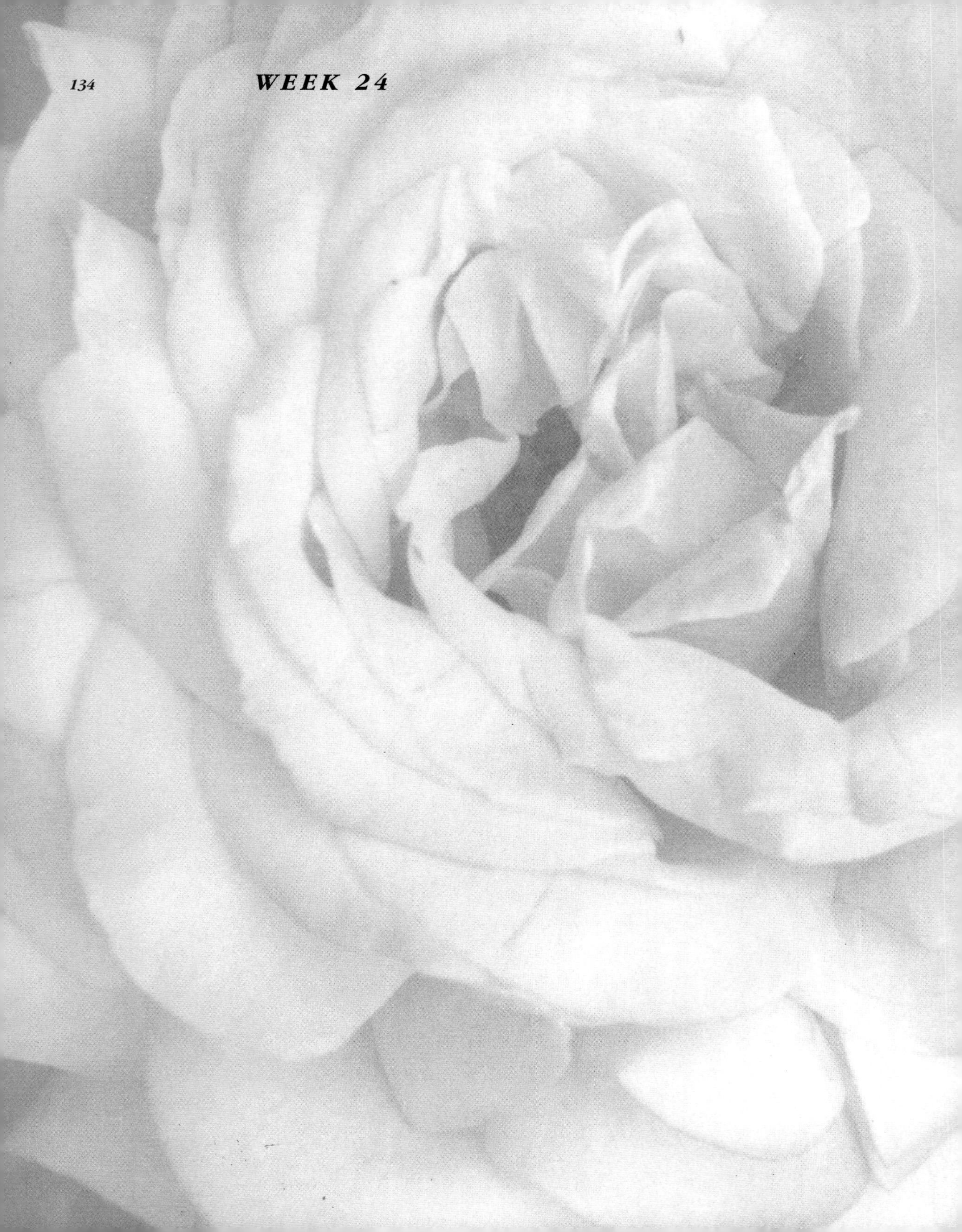

When you embrace a tree you are accepting the gift of pure air, the vitality of life its essence has prepared for you.

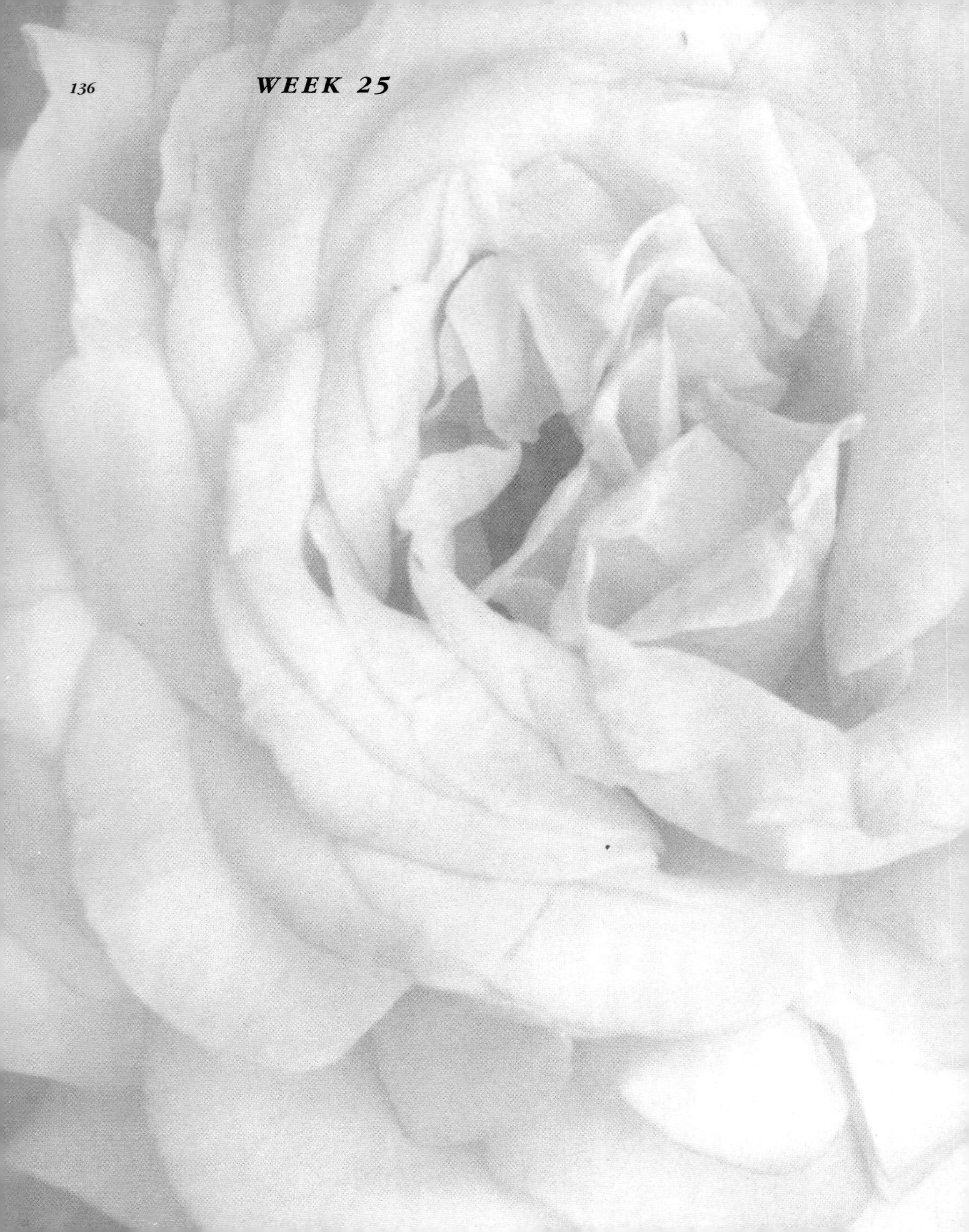

The difference between judgment and discrimination is the difference between seeing with blinders and seeing clearly.

The way to change the world is to change yourself.

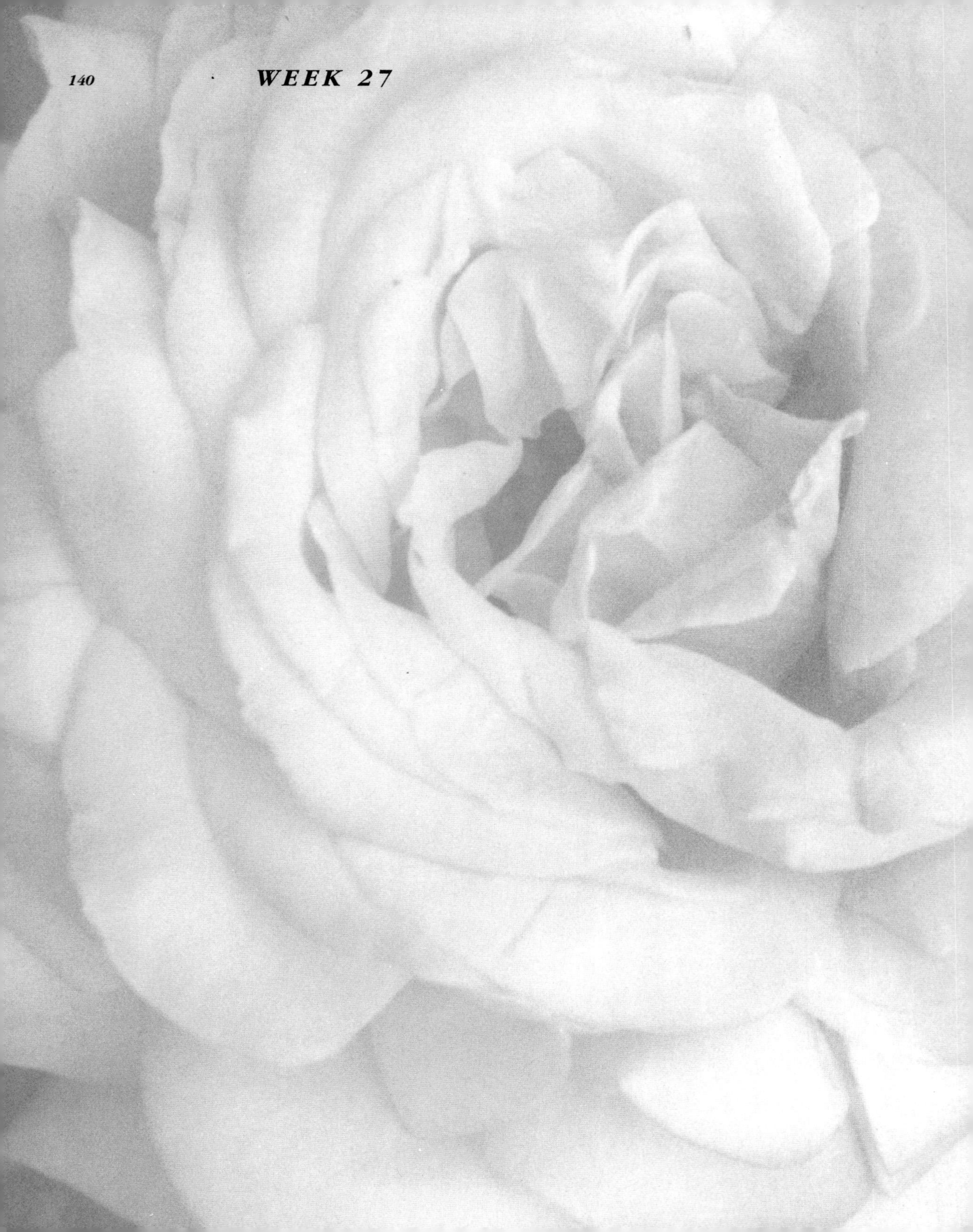

In lifting yourself you also lift others.

There is strength in union.

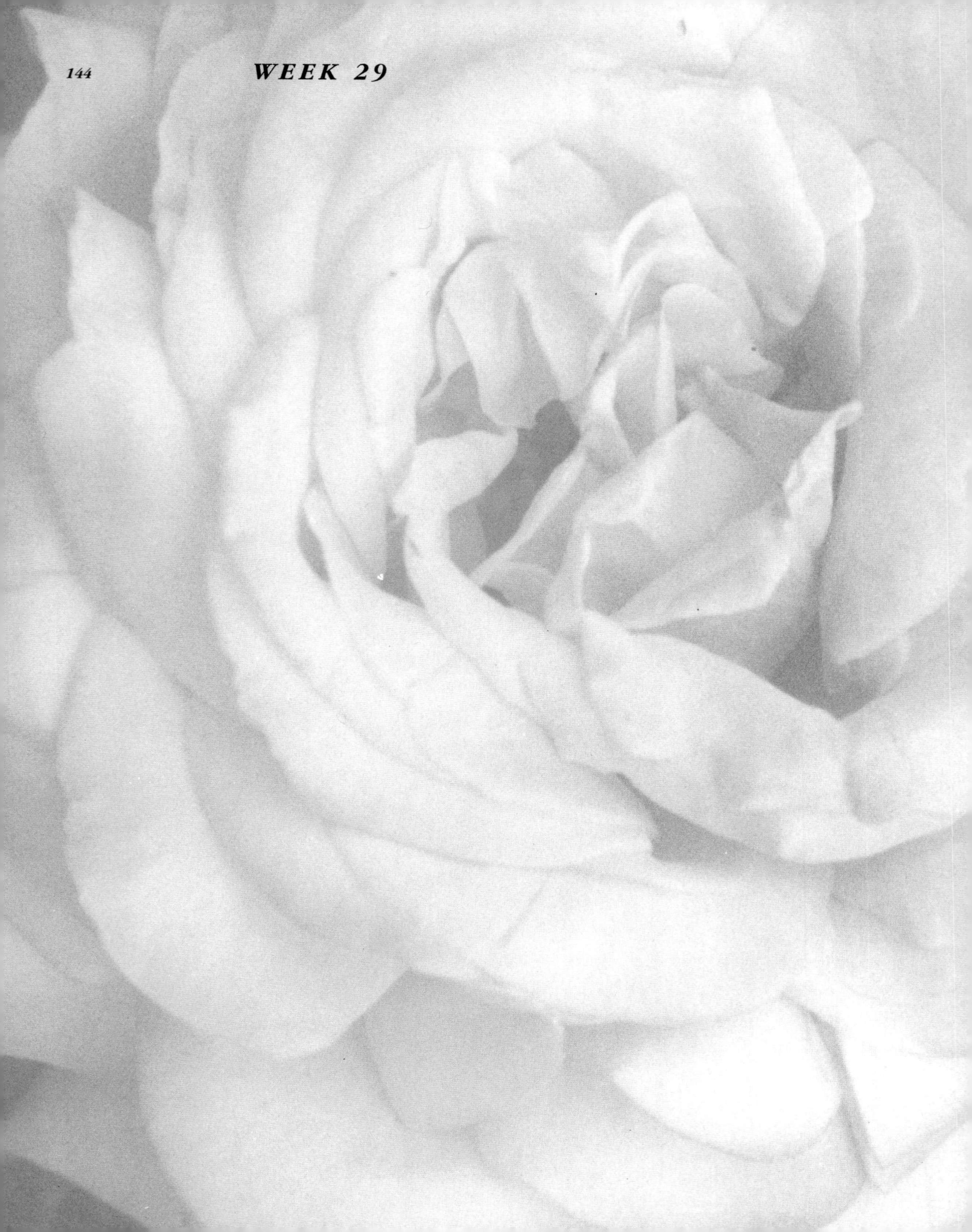

Excuses are a way of avoiding being responsible for your actions.

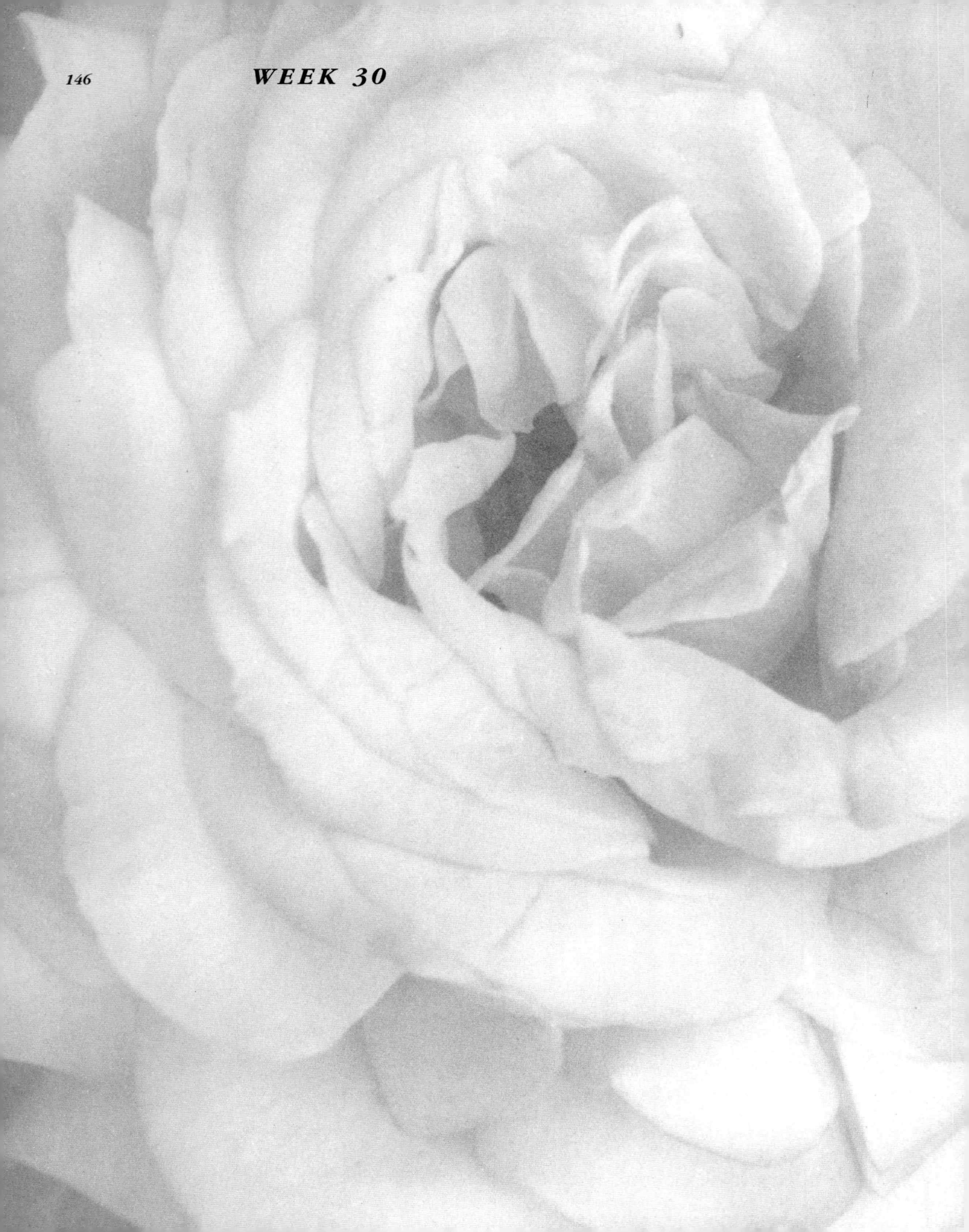

No person stands alone in the universe.

WEEK 31

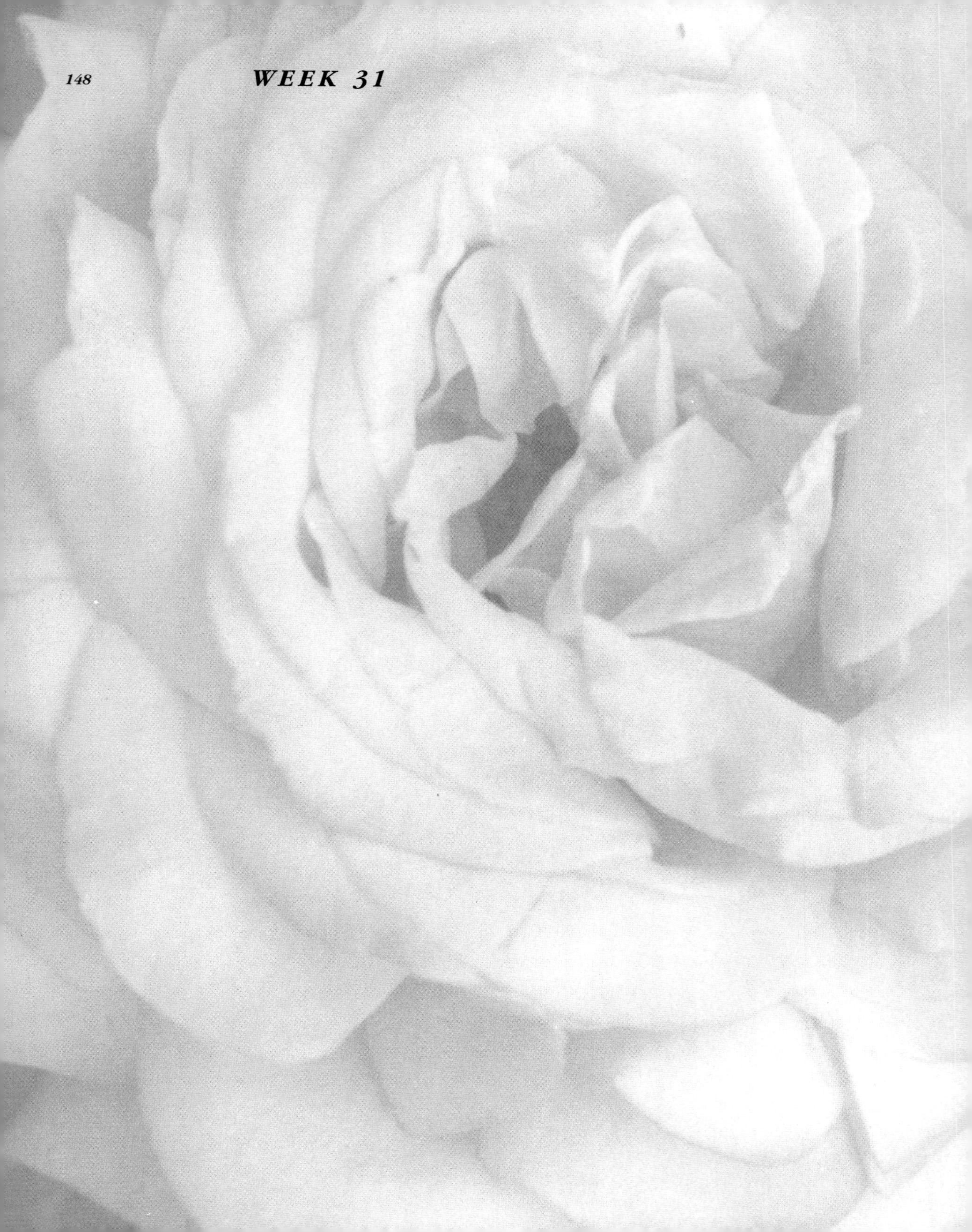

As I see myself is as I see others.

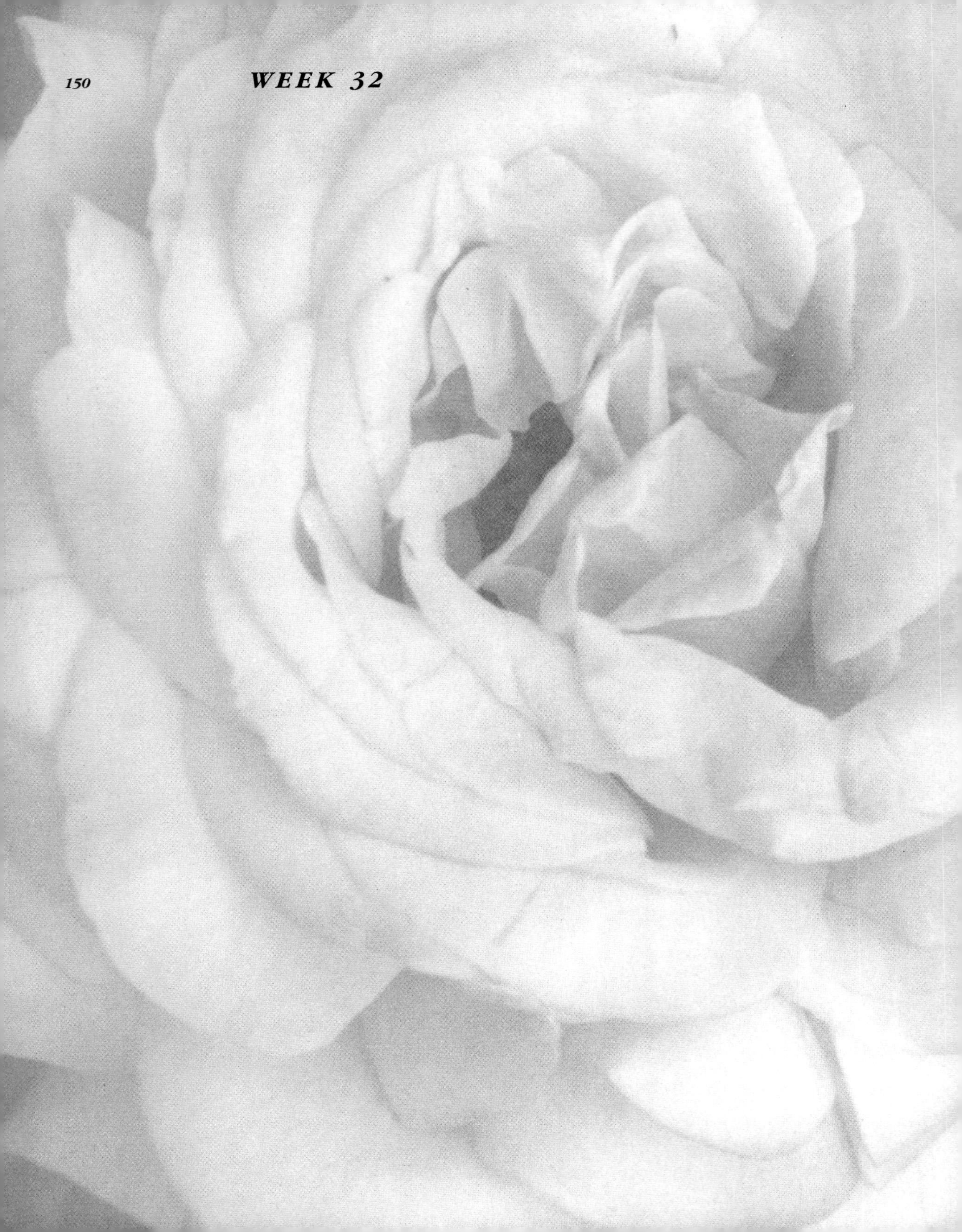

Perseverance furthers.

WEEK 33

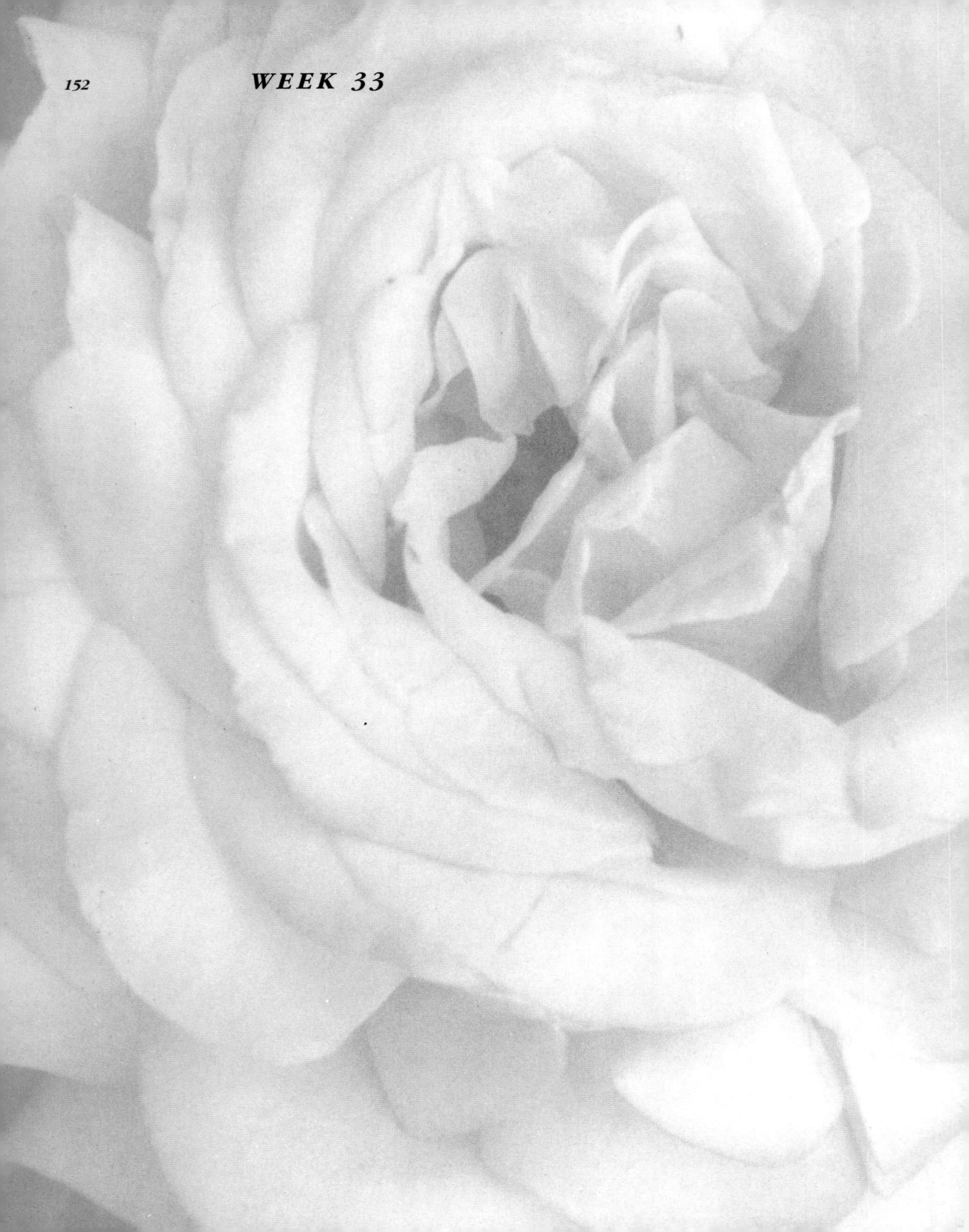

Although some things may appear to be solid, the essence of all things, formed and unformed, is pure energy.

WEEK 34

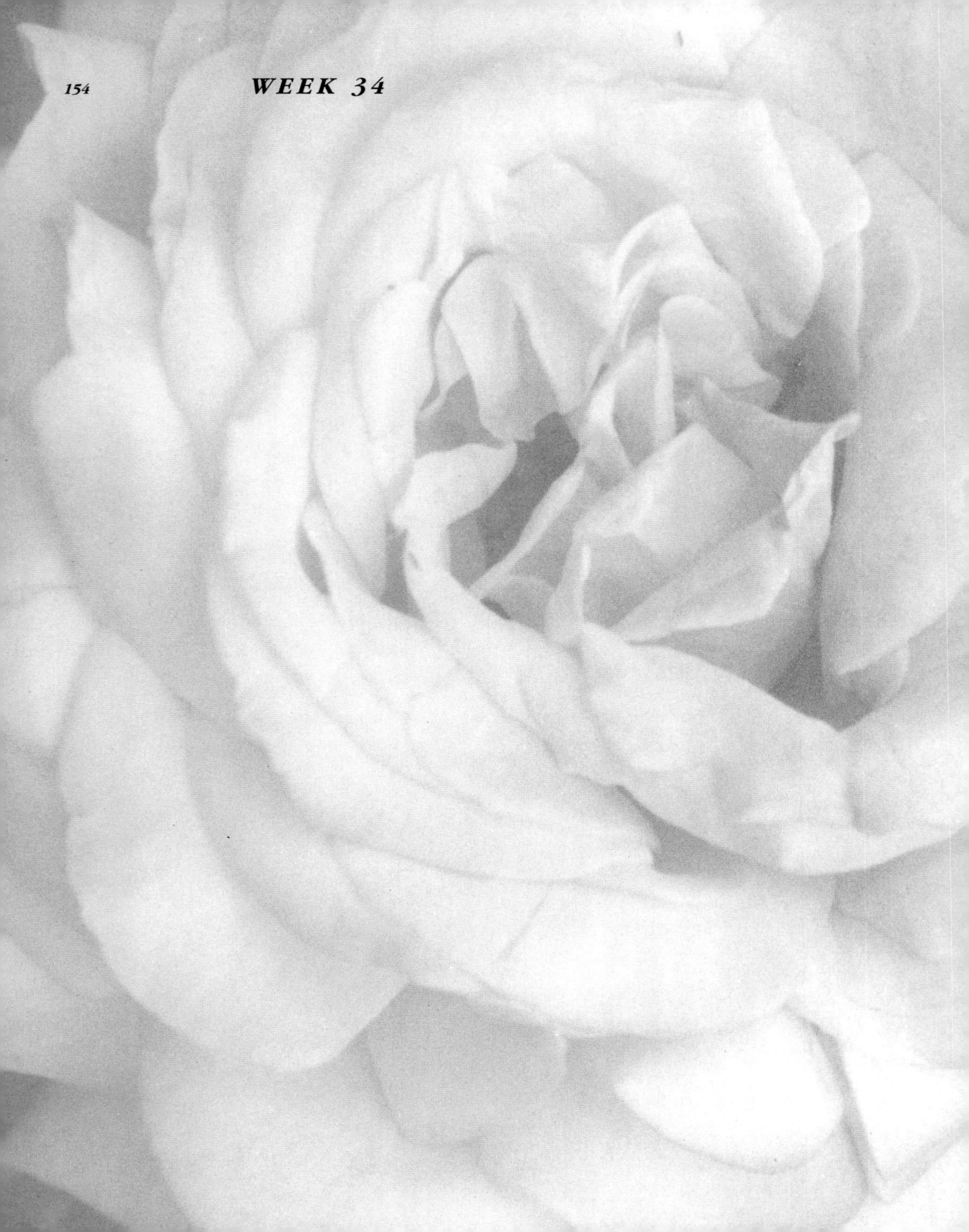

The size of the vessel determines how much it can hold, and size is solely an image created by the mind.

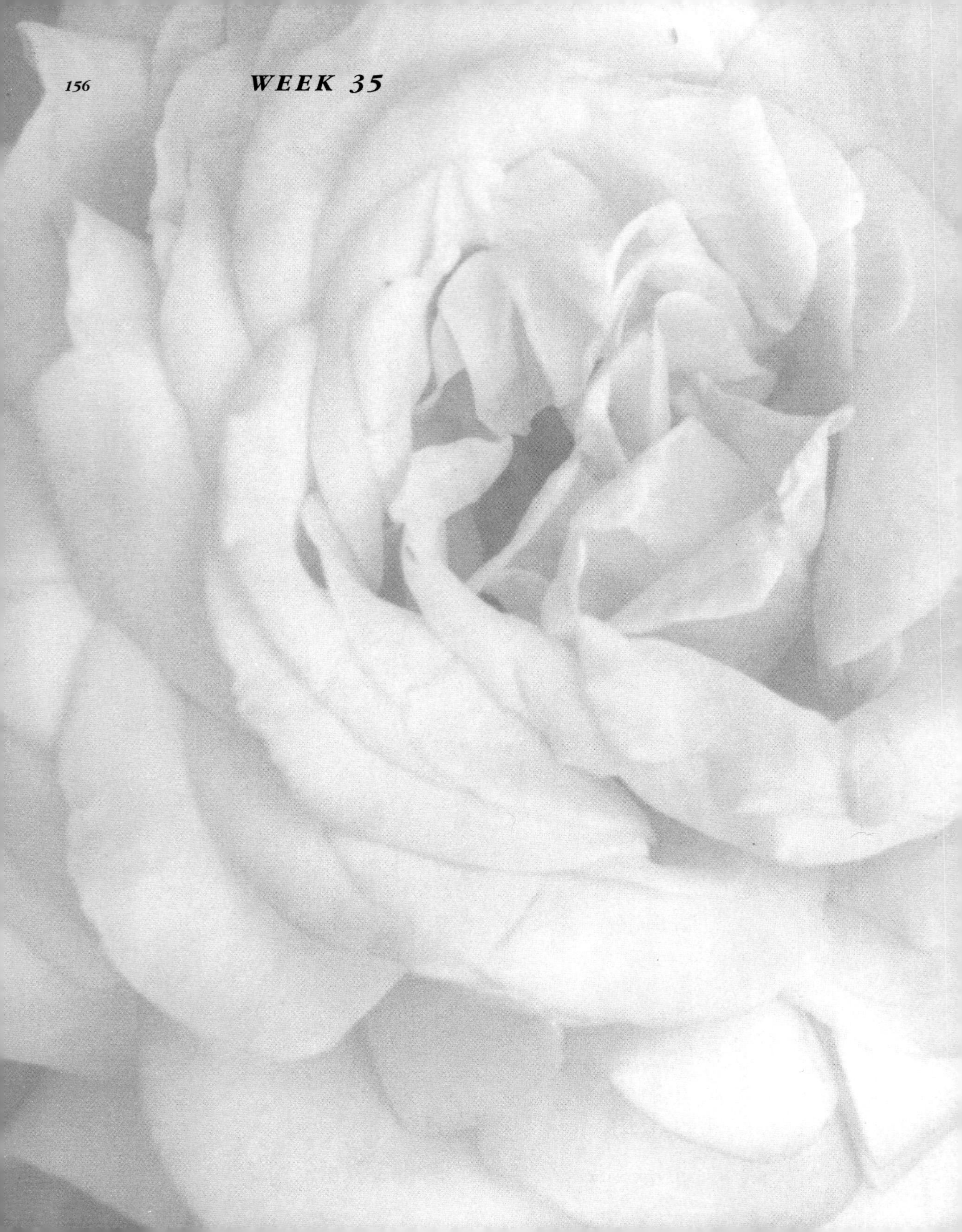

In reaching for the stars, I stretch myself to infinity.

WEEK 36

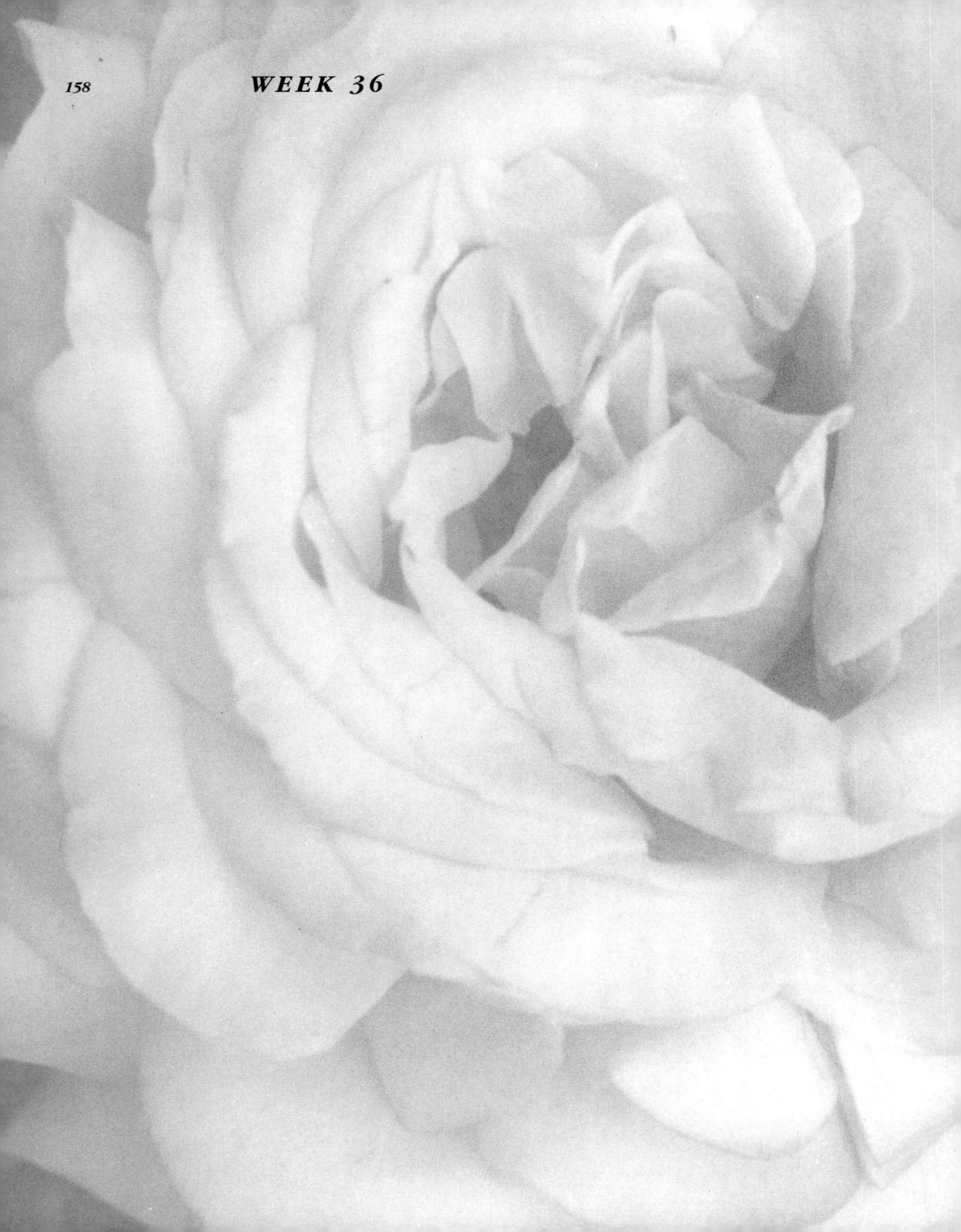

To focus on differences is to divert attention from unity.

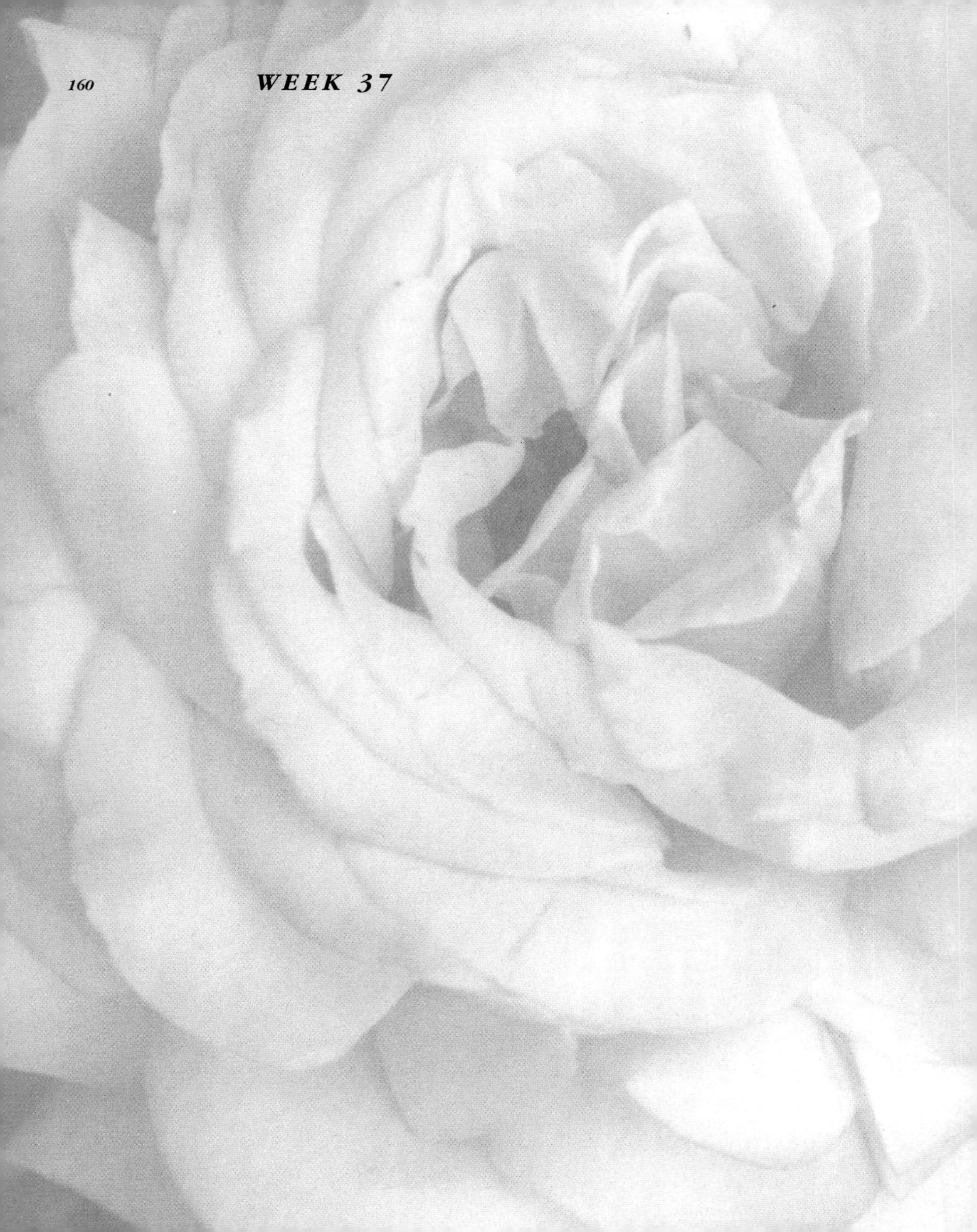

Energy follows attention.

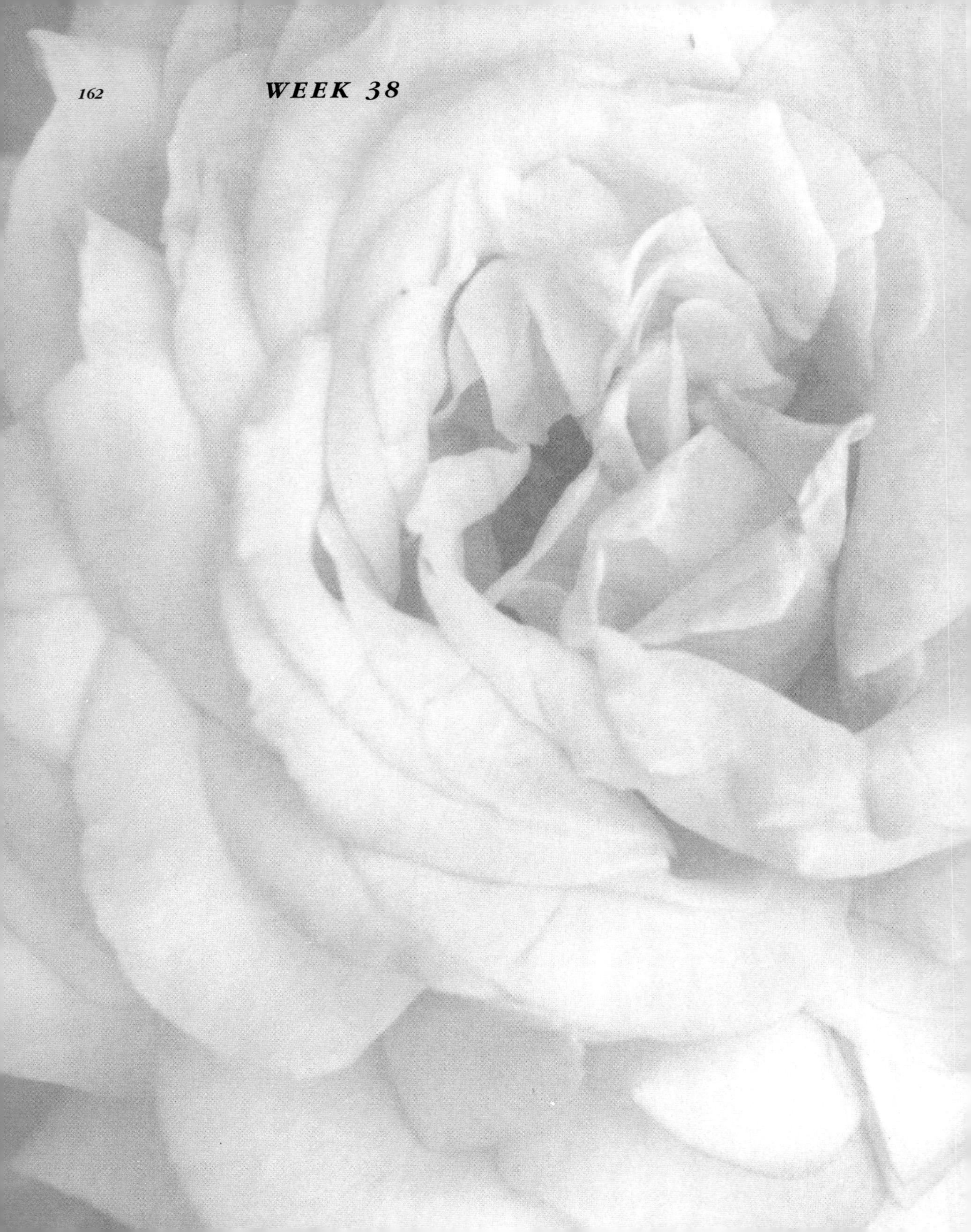

*The growth and blossoming of a soul unfolds in a defined and orderly
pattern within a time that has its own clock.*

WEEK 39

Similar vibrations attract.

WEEK 40

In loving myself more fully, I am able to love others more fully.

Surrendering to life releases the brakes on your growth.

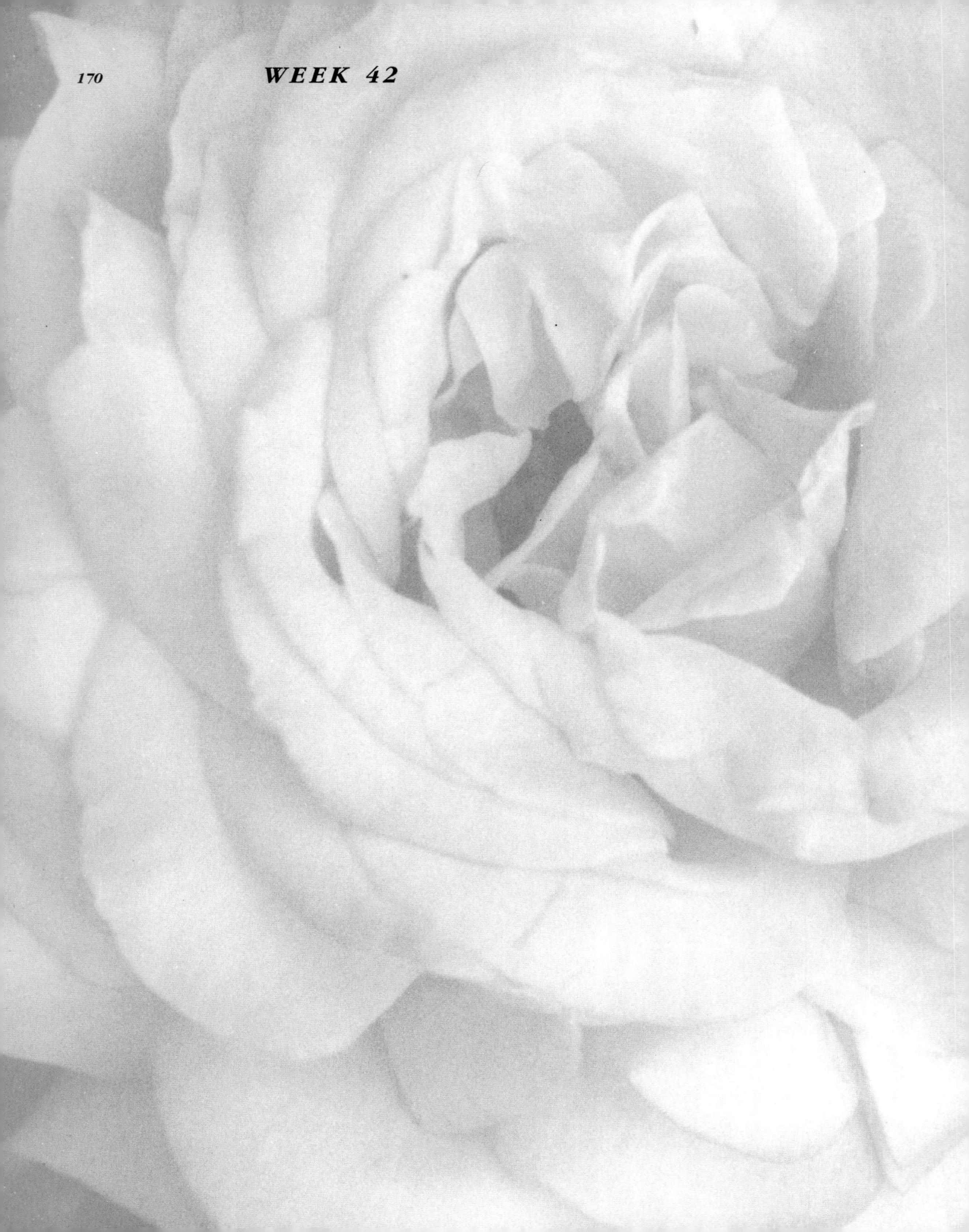

A river flows, sometimes faster through the rapid narrows, sometimes slower in the wider deltas, but it always flows.

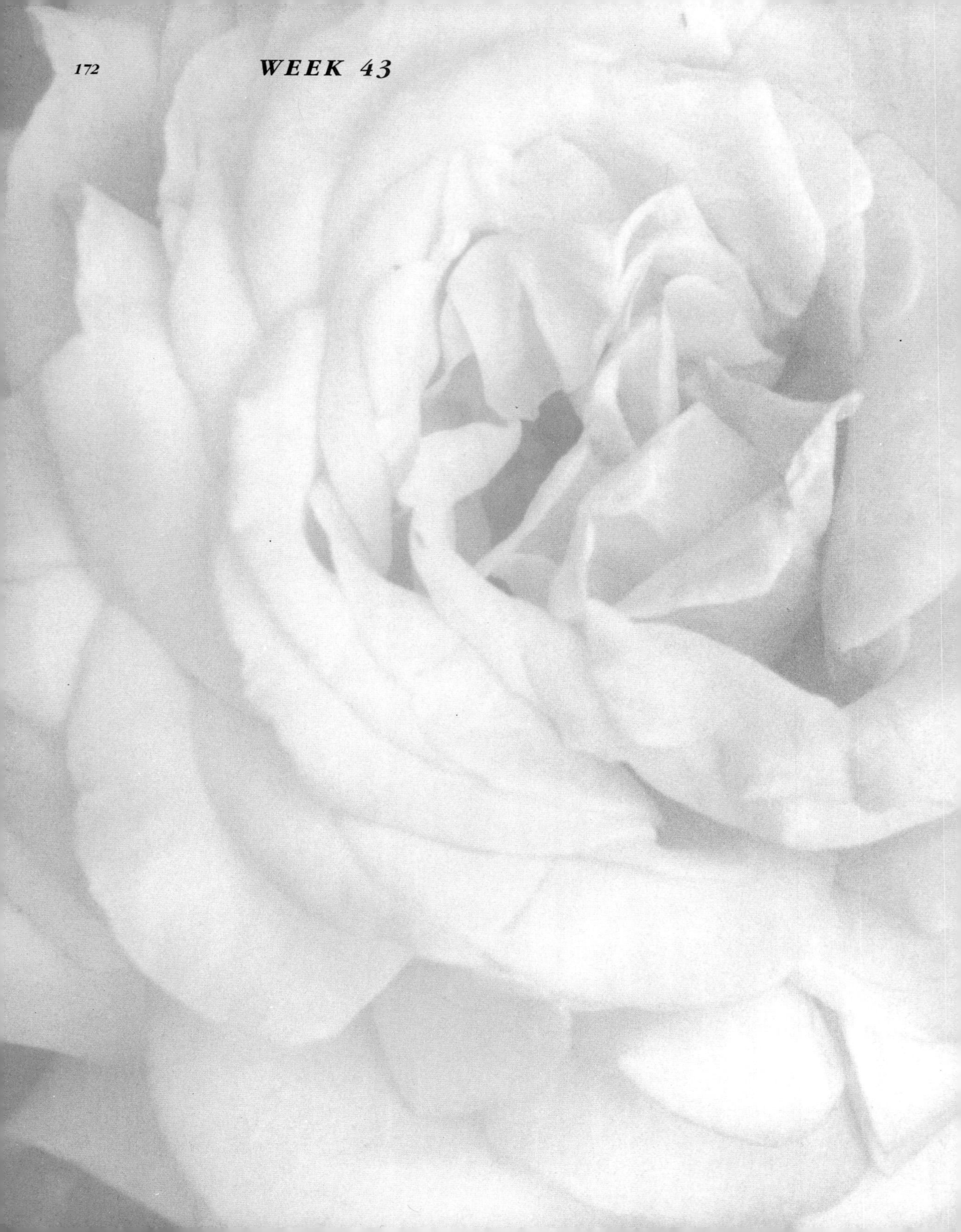

If you look at the glass as half full, you look with the consciousness of prosperity; if you look at the glass as half empty, you look with the consciousness of scarcity.

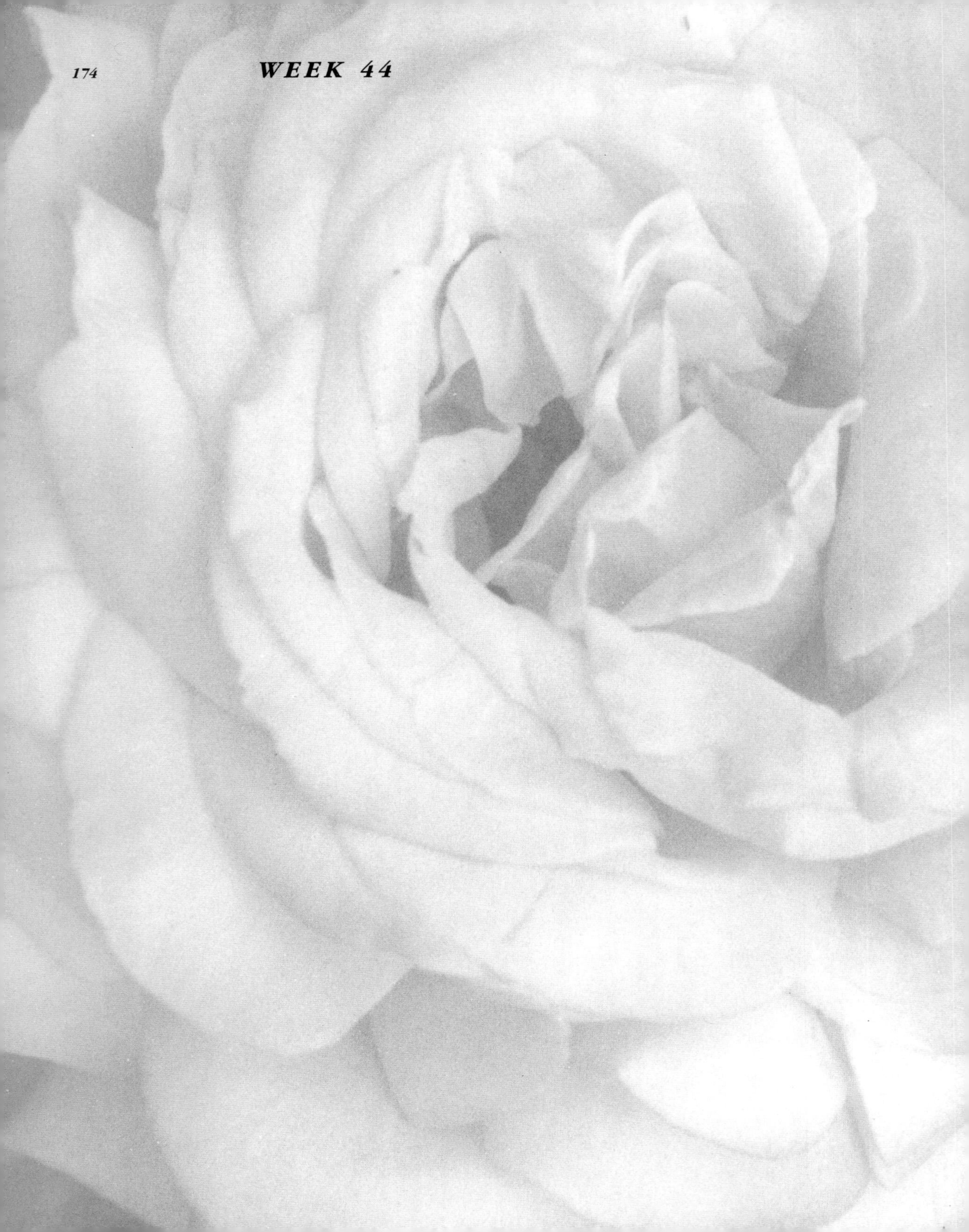

Do what is in front of you with full awareness, and everything else will take care of itself.

WEEK 45

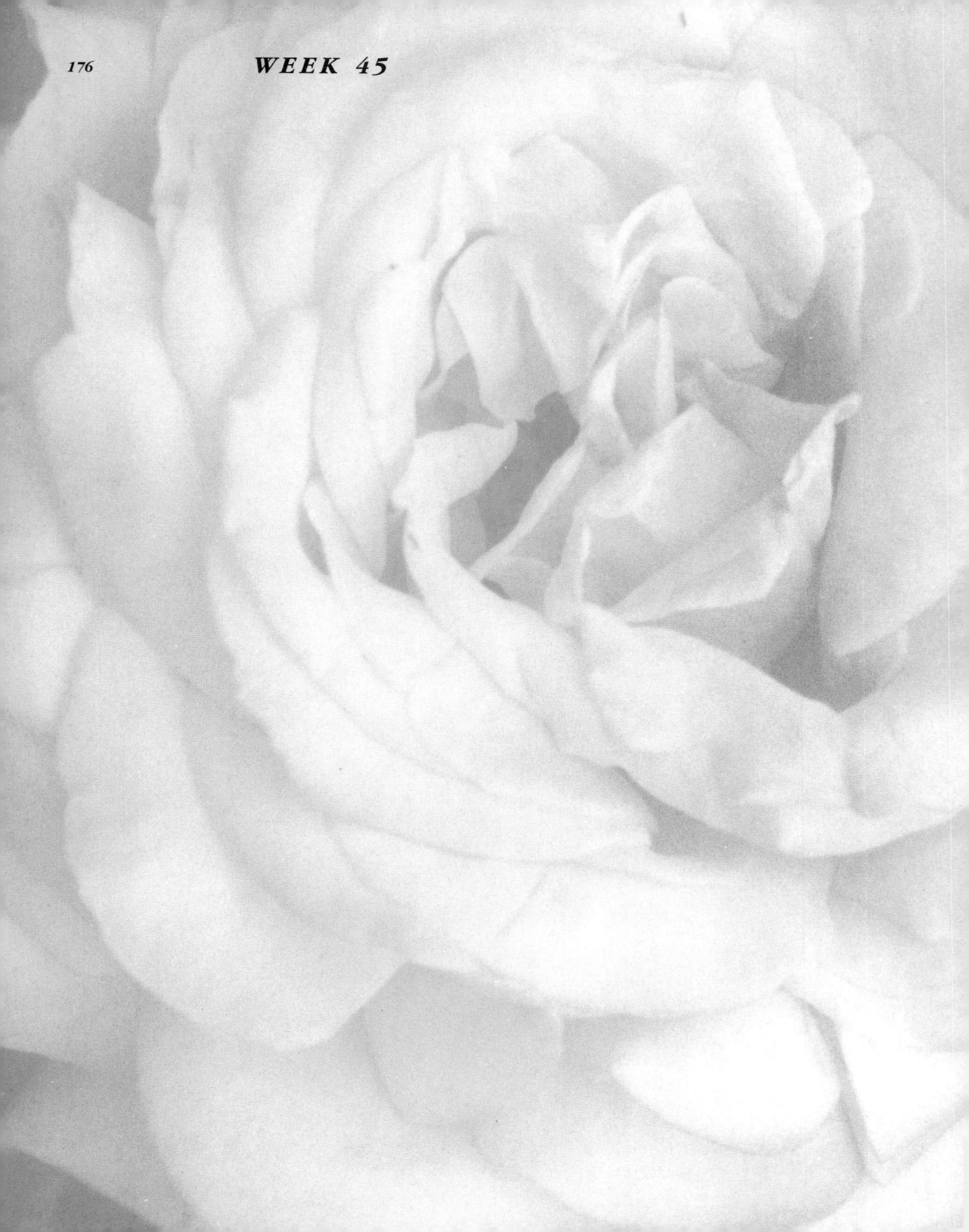

The how and the why of the journey is of greater significance than the destination.

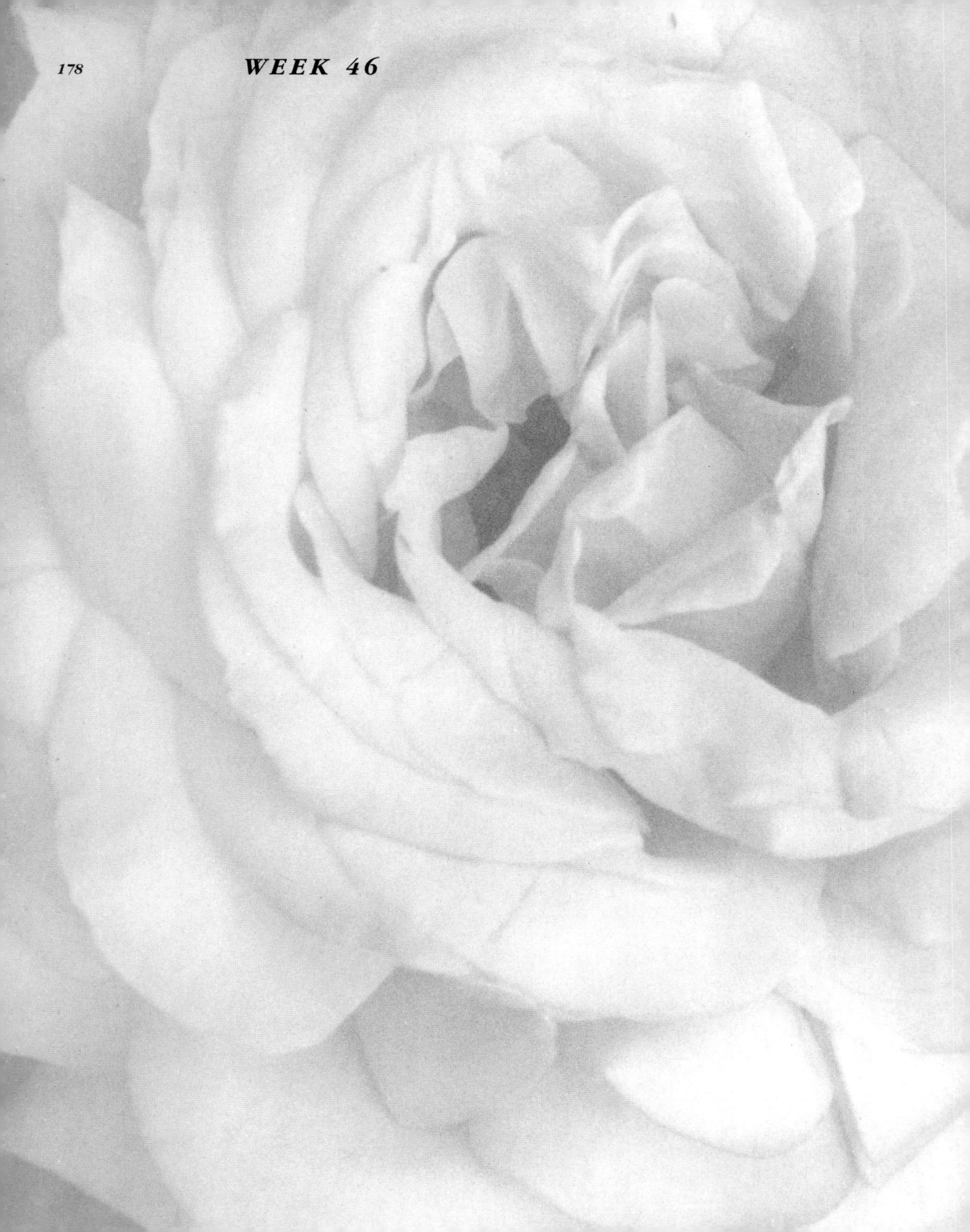

In caring for yourself first, you can care better for others.

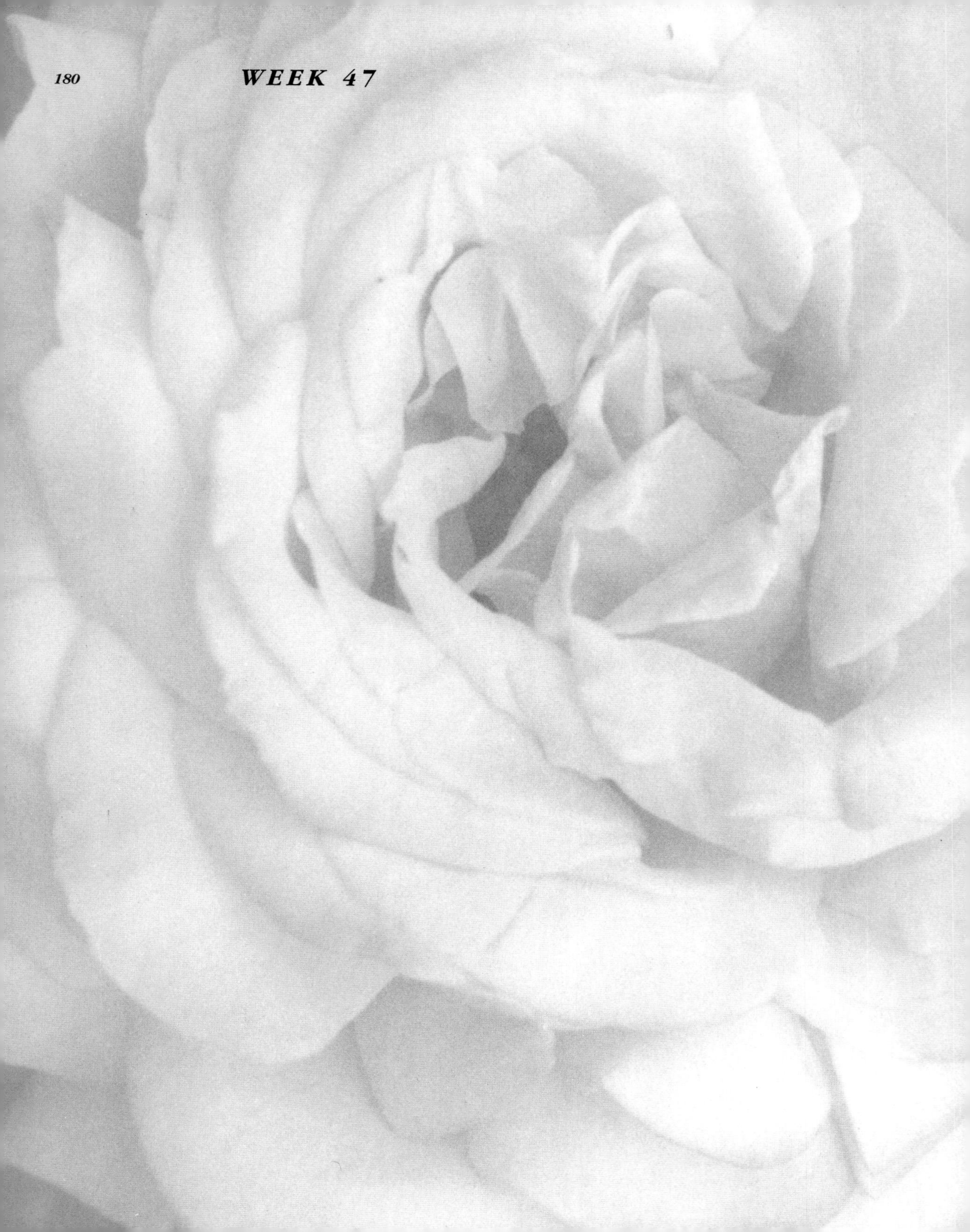

Life is a series of moments; fully experience each one.

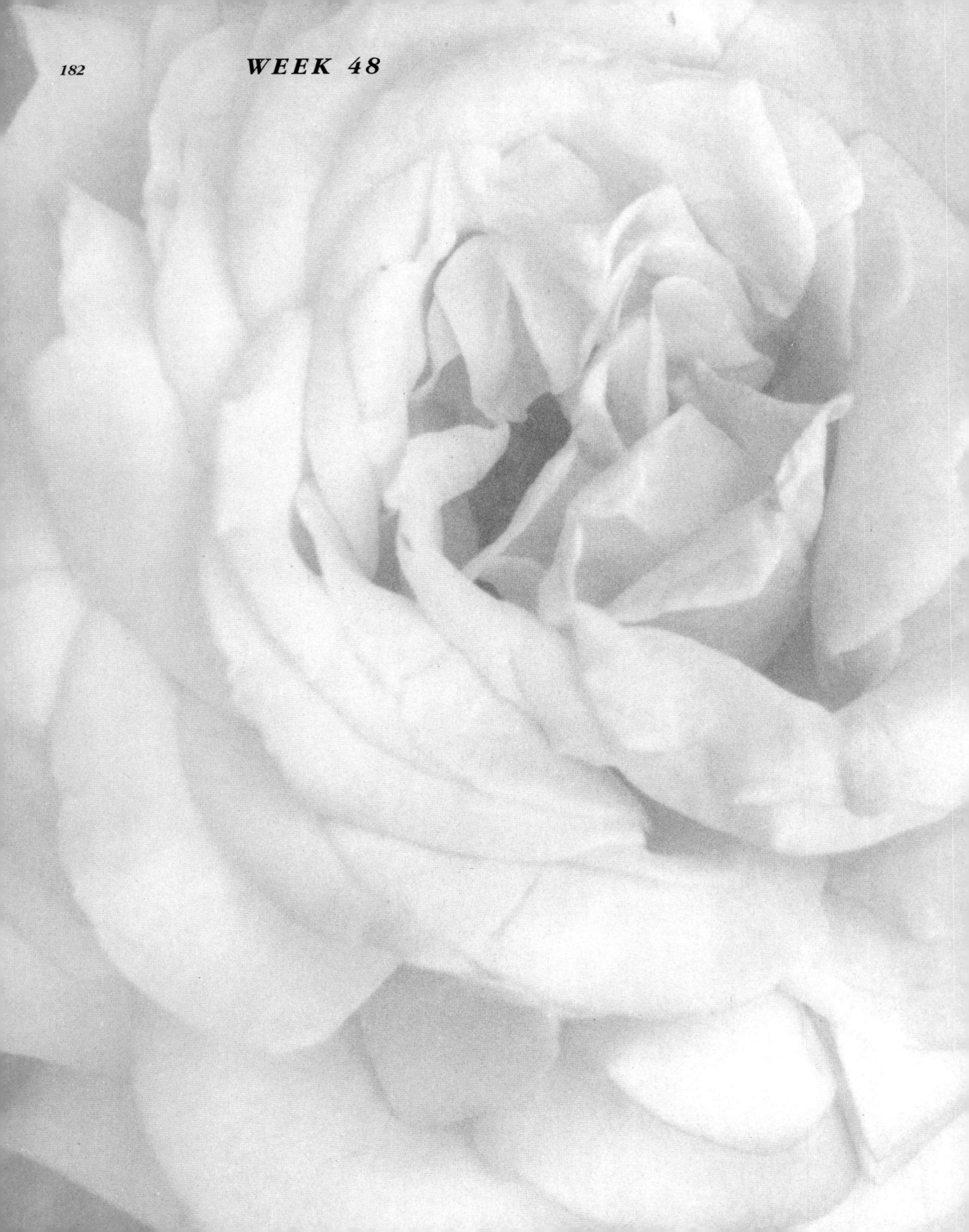

A mandala reflects the synergistic beauty of wholeness.

WEEK 49

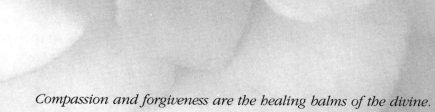

Compassion and forgiveness are the healing balms of the divine.

WEEK 50

Heaven on earth is when the sacred merges with the human.

WEEK 51

When I know that everyone is an individualized expression of the divine, I know that the unity of all beings is a reality.

WEEK 52

Be gentle, loving, and compassionate with yourself.